BASIC STUDENT MINISTRY
in THE KINGDOM-FOCUSED CHURCH

COMPILED BY
DWAYNE C. ULMER

LifeWay Press
Nashville, Tennessee

© Copyright 2003 • LifeWay Press
All rights reserved

No part of this work may be reproduced or transmitted in any form or by any means, electronic or mechanical, including photocopying and recording, or by any information storage or retrieval system, except as may be expressly permitted in writing by the publisher. Requests for permission should be addressed in writing to LifeWay Press, One LifeWay Plaza, Nashville, TN 37234-0174.

ISBN 0-6330-9038-7

This book is the text for course LS-0523 in the subject area "Ministry"
in the Christian Growth Study Plan.

Dewey Decimal Classification Number 259.24
Subject Heading: CHURCH WORK WITH STUDENTS\STUDENT MINISTRIES

Printed in the United States of America.

To order additional copies of this resource: WRITE LifeWay Church Resources Customer Service, One LifeWay Plaza, Nashville, TN 37234-0113; FAX orders to (615) 251-5933; E-MAIL to *CustomerService@lifeway.com;* ONLINE at *www.lifeway.com;* or visit the LifeWay Christian Store serving you.

Graphic Design: Edward Crawford

Student Ministry Publishing
LifeWay Christian Resources
of the Southern Baptist Convention
One LifeWay Plaza
Nashville, TN 37234-0174

Unless otherwise noted, Scripture quotations are from the *Holman Christian Standard Bible®,* copyright © 1999, 2000, 2002, 2004 by Holman Bible Publishers. Used by permission.

Contents

4 Writers
5 Foreword
6 Introduction
11 Chapter 1: Evangelism
31 Chapter 2: Discipleship
47 Chapter 3: Fellowship
65 Chapter 4: Ministry
81 Chapter 5: Worship
99 Chapter 6: Administration
123 Appendix 1: FAITH
124 Appendix 2: Checklist for Evaluating Bible Study Resources
125 Appendix 3: Safety and Legal Issues
126 Appendix 4: Mission Statement
127 Appendix 5: Job Description (Sample)

Christian Growth Study Plan

Writer Bios

Introduction
Dwayne C. Ulmer, Ed.D., is the managing director of Student Ministry Publishing at LifeWay Christian Resources in Nashville, Tennessee. He has more than 20 years of youth ministry experience and has served as a volunteer youth worker, a bi-vocational youth minister, and full-time youth minister at churches in Texas and Tennessee. He has also been an adjunct youth ministry professor. Dwayne is married to Beverly and has three boys, Kevin and Kyle age 8 and Eric age 1. He and his family attend Una Baptist Church in Antioch, Tennessee, where Dwayne serves as a youth leader and currently is the interim youth minister.

Chapter 1—Evangelism
Wesley Black, Ph.D., is professor of youth/student ministry, Southwestern Baptist Theological Seminary, Fort Worth, Texas. Wes and his wife Sandi have two grown children and one granddaughter. Wes has been involved in youth ministry for more than 36 years.

Chapter 2—Discipleship
Karen E. Jones, Ph.D., is associate professor of Christian education at Golden Gate Baptist Theological Seminary in San Francisco, California, and is the head of the Educational Ministries department at Huntington College in Huntington, Indiana. She served as a youth minister for more than 15 years in churches in Missouri and Texas and continues to coordinate youth mission trips with the North American and International Mission Boards. Karen has been a youth discipleship curriculum writer for more than 20 years and has co-authored or contributed chapters to several books on youth ministry. Her husband, Dennis, is a freelance illustrator. They have two sons, Nick, a junior at Oklahoma Baptist University, and Pete, a junior at Huntington North High School.

Chapter 3—Fellowship
Rick Morton, Ph.D., is assistant professor of leadership and church ministry at The Southern Baptist Theological Seminary in Louisville, Kentucky, where he teaches in the area of youth ministry. He has been a student minister in churches in Tennessee and Louisiana, and is a frequent youth ministry conference leader. He is married to Denise, and they currently volunteer in the student ministry of Highview Baptist Church in Louisville.

Chapter 4—Ministry
Allen Jackson, Ph.D., is associate professor of youth education at the New Orleans Baptist Theological Seminary and the director of the Youth Ministry Institute. He has been a youth minister at churches in Louisiana and Georgia, and has served in various other staff positions as an interim minister. He and his wife Judi are parents of two millennials, Aaron and Sarah, and currently volunteer as youth workers at the First Baptist Church of New Orleans.

Chapter 5—Worship
Scott H. Stevens, Ph.D., has 20 years of youth ministry experience and has served as a volunteer youth worker, a part-time and full-time youth minister, and a youth ministry professor. He currently serves as an editor in chief in Student Ministry Publishing at LifeWay Christian Resources where he develops materials for youth ministers and youth workers. Scott is married to Debbie and has two children, Tanner age 9 and Annie age 5. His family attends Forest Hills Baptist Church in Franklin, Tennessee, where Scott serves as a volunteer youth worker.

Chapter 6—Administration
Richard Ross, Ph.D., is professor of youth/student ministry, Southwestern Baptist Theological Seminary in Fort Worth, Texas. He served as minister of youth in churches for almost 30 years and presently is a volunteer youth leader at Wedgwood Baptist Church in Fort Worth. He served as youth ministry consultant for LifeWay Christian Resources from 1984–2000. He serves as a spokesperson for the True Love Waits campaign and has written or compiled 20 books on youth ministry. He is married to LaJuana, a lifetime youth leader, and is father to Clayton, a teenager.

Foreword

WHAT AN OPPORTUNITY! You are so fortunate! You are about to embark on a journey that will impact your ministry and provide you a kingdom perspective. And you get to travel with the best! In *Basic Student Ministry,* you will share the experience and expertise of several of the top student ministry leaders around today: Richard Ross, Allen Jackson, Karen Jones, Wes Black, Scott Stevens, and Rick Morton. As compiler, Dwayne Ulmer has blended the best to provide you valuable insights and direction.

In this single volume, these dedicated youth leaders point you to the basics. Keep in mind this question as you journey through the book: When you strip away all the bells and whistles, what really matters in student ministry? Whether you are a pastor looking for help with your church's youth, or a youth minister just getting started, the information on the following pages will provide a solid foundation for your ministry.

May God bring insight into your life on what it means to have a kingdom-focused student ministry.

Jimmy Hester, Senior Director
Student Ministry Publishing
LifeWay Church Resources

Introduction
Dwayne C. Ulmer

REFLECTING BACK ON MY DAYS IN YOUTH MINISTRY as a teenager, I get nothing but warm feelings. It was a time of an intense flurry of activity in which I was fully engaged. Every time there was an activity or event I was there and got the T-shirt. We had a lot fun and I'm sure I learned a lot. I had a great group of friends and we got rowdy occasionally, at least enough to rile and frustrate my youth minister, but we were always there. It's really kind of funny now that I think about it. When I graduated I fell away from the church. It didn't seem to be as interesting of a place anymore and it certainly wasn't fun. I kind of went through a spiritual searching phase for a while. It has only been recently that I have begun to get back into church. Even still, things seem kind of dry at the church I have been attending.

—*Jon, 26*
Norfolk, Virginia

MY TIME IN YOUTH MINISTRY WAS A LABORATORY for my life. I grew so much during those teenage years. My youth leaders made a huge investment in my life and I grew from being a shallow and selfish Christian to an enthusiastic, evangelistic minister. I was challenged to think for myself and develop a biblical worldview. I developed deep and passionate personal convictions and a clear sense of right and wrong. I was afforded opportunities to do missions and practice sharing my faith and even saw some of my closest friends come to know Christ. I learned how to have a personal walk with Christ that has carried me through my young adult years. Even now, the priority of my life, other than my wife, is the ministry I have through my church.

—*James, 28*
Baton Rouge, Louisiana

YOUTH MINISTRY IS AN OVERWHELMING TASK to say the least. When you contemplate the necessity of ministering to teenagers in the midst of the violent changes existing in their adolescent developmental stages, the complexity of youth cultures in which those changes are taking place, the nature and makeup of the various family components of teenagers, and the responsibilities and expectations of youth ministry positions in a variety of churches, things can get complicated and confusing very quickly. The big questions are: *What is youth ministry, really? How does one develop and lead a "successful" youth ministry? Then, given that a church has a person who is called and has agreed to give leadership to the youth ministry either in a paid role or as a volunteer, how does that person lead a group of students from a status of being lost without Christ to a reproducing, kingdom-focused Christian, whose faith is dynamic and growing, especially when the youth minister or volunteer leader may have limited education and experience?*

Because these questions are so hard, complex, and even terrifying, most youth ministers, if not all of them from time to time, settle into the path of least resistance, especially if they lack training and experience in their roles. When under the gun and expectations are high, it is logical that they will become more concerned about survival than actually taking the time to evaluate their approach and think strategically about how to plan and implement biblically-based ministries. Many simply become more concerned with filling up the church calendar with the hottest new program or event with only a slight glance at the overall health of their ministries or spiritual development of their students. Few are concerned about discovering weaknesses and fixing what's broken because they feel the pressure of competing with the church across town or the high profile ministry in another state that seems to have all the answers to difficult youth ministry questions wrapped in a nice, neat package. For these reasons, this book attempts to celebrate the simplicity of the youth minister's work. It is a call back to the basics and a challenge to examine the foundation of youth ministry. This work has a threefold purpose: (1) to identify and define the biblical functions of youth ministry within the context of the local church so that youth ministers will know what they are supposed to do; (2) to provide some basic principles of work that will enable youth ministers to think strategically about their ministry; and (3) to offer ideas and suggestions for how to improve and accomplish these biblical functions within the context of a local church.

Practically speaking, youth ministry defined is all that a local church does within the context of a community that addresses the needs of teenagers (usually grades seven through twelve), their parents and families, and their adult leaders. For the purpose of this work, the terms *youth ministry* and *student ministry* will both be used, though generally speaking student ministry can be broader in that it includes collegiate ministry as well as youth ministry. "Student ministry," however, within the current culture has come to be associated with youth ministry. Consequently the terms *youth*, *teenagers*, *teens*, *students*, and *adolescents* will also be used interchangeably. This work is for the youth minister, youth leader, volunteer leader, youth director, youth pastor, or youth committee member—anyone who may have a responsibility for the teenagers in their churches whether he or she is paid as a full-time staff member, part-time staff member, bivocational leader, or volunteer youth lay leader.

Youth ministry success over the years has been based on the easy and obvious indicators: the number of teenagers baptized, the number of youth in attendance, the size of the youth group, the number and nature of youth activities, and the size of the budget that drives a youth ministry emphasis. But are those healthy success markers? Wouldn't a youth group that promoted out a huge number of high school graduates and replaced them with a significantly smaller class of incoming seventh graders go down in attendance? What about the church that baptized a large number of teenagers but whose average Sunday School attendance went down? Would it be considered growing or declining? What about the rural church that averages only half a dozen teenagers in Sunday School? Is it fair to compare its ministry to a church in a highly populated suburban area? And then there is the question of spiritual maturity. Are the teenagers involved in a youth ministry growing in faith? Are the teenagers sharing their faith? Is the youth ministry actually making a difference for the kingdom of God in the surrounding community and at the local secondary schools? Are the needs of the teenagers' parents and families being addressed? Such answers are a little more difficult to come by than the numbers recorded by most churches in their annual reports.

Results

The age-old question most youth ministers would like to ask is, *When we get where we are going, where will we be?* In his book, *Kingdom Principles for Church Growth,* Gene Mims defines the 1-5-4 principle and argues that it is the key to church growth—getting where you need to be. It should be noted that true church growth is never the result of methods. It is the result of the supernatural activity of God. When the church recognizes and applies kingdom principles in the power of the Holy Spirit, however, increases in church growth will naturally follow. Mims' principle points to one great commission, five church functions (evangelism, discipleship, fellowship, ministry, and worship), and four results in church growth. When the Great Commission is carried out through the five functions in the power of the Holy Spirit, Mims suggests there will be four dimensions of church growth. The same four results should be evident in a healthy youth ministry. They will indicate where a youth ministry needs to be. These four results act like the legs of a table. In harmony with the other three, each leg helps achieve the right result. One extra-long leg by itself will not make up for a deficit in the others. Real growth, kingdom-focused growth, will be exhibited in all four areas according to God's perfect will.[1]

Numerical Growth.—The first of these is numerical growth. Obviously there are a multitude of Scriptures that show the New Testament church grew numerically. But what does that mean exactly? To be sure, numerical growth by itself can be deceptive. If a youth ministry, for example, records a large number of baptisms, it would be easy to think the program is evangelistic and thus be evaluated as healthy. A question to ask, however, is how many of these folks are still coming and growing as disciples? A "large number" is also relative. In a small community, a large number may be five or six a year. In a larger community, 150 a year may be a small number. Also, if a youth ministry is drawing a large crowd consistently, it might be easy to assume the ministry is healthy. But what kinds of ministry and mission projects is the youth ministry doing and are the large numbers maturing spiritually? Still, numerical growth is a dimension of healthy church growth, especially since every number represents a life.[2] Some things youth ministries can look at that would indicate numerical growth could be to compare the ending average attendance in various youth ministry programs to the average attendance at the beginning of the year. Youth ministers could also look at the ending Sunday School membership as compared to the beginning Sunday School membership. Numerical growth might also be observed in the growth of small group Bible study units. Of course the number of baptisms can also be a sign of numerical growth.

Spiritual Transformation.—Another dimension of church growth is spiritual growth, or in other words, spiritual transformation. Christ had no intention for kingdom growth to be shallow and for believers to have to continue to be spoon-fed spiritual truths. Christian teenagers who are a part of a local church body ought to be maturing in their relationship with Christ, developing in their relationships with other believers, developing relationships with the unsaved, and developing Christian discipline.[3] This concept is known as spiritual transformation, which is "God's work of changing a believer into the likeness of Jesus by creating a new identity in Christ and by empowering a lifelong relationship of love, trust, and obedience to glorify God."[4] Though this dimension of growth in a youth ministry might be a little more difficult to identify, there are still some things a youth minister can look for that might indicate spiritual growth.

Paul Borthwick says youth ministers can do this in two ways. The first is through short-term results. He says youth ministers can look for an increase in "significant spiritual markers." Spiritual markers are things like memorizing Scripture, reading the Bible regularly, spending time in daily devotions, completing discipleship courses, sharing Christ with friends, participating in service/ministry projects, reading Christian books, sharing personal testimonies, and joining the church. Though these spiritual markers would not be a hard and fast checklist to measure spiritual maturity, certainly they are indicators. He also says there will be some long-term results. He argues that it often takes time for our ministry investments with students to bear fruit. According to Borthwick, this will be indicative of folks returning to the youth minister to thank him or her years later for their equipping.[5] Teenagers who end up in full-time ministry or involved in church leadership roles as adults would also be indicative of long-term results. Some other things youth ministers might look for would be clear evidence students are becoming Great Commission Christians, youth who are involved in leadership training, an increase in the percentage of youth who are participating in evangelism training or mission involvement, youth who are choosing to engage in dynamic and meaningful corporate and private worship experiences, and youth who are asking probing and significant questions. Spiritual transformation can be seen in the way individual students relate to Christ, other believers, and lost teenagers.

Ministry Expansion.—Church growth will also be reflected in ministry expansion—teenagers will become more sensitive to the needs of the fellowship, the community, and the world. Youth will recognize their giftedness, discover power for ministry through the Holy Spirit, and see a larger amount of ministry taking place where service and care are clearly evident.[6] Some other things to look for in the area of ministry expansion would be: an increase in the number of ministries provided or sponsored by the youth ministry, an increase in the approximate number of youth engaging in ministry, an increase in the approximate amount of youth money supporting community ministry action, more effective strategies for impacting and ministering to the parents and families of teenagers, and an increase in the approximate number of youth involved in campus ministry. Much of the growth in the area of ministry may also come at the hands of the teenagers themselves who are stepping up to meet the needs around them without the prompting of adult leadership.

Kingdom Advance.—Kingdom advance is the fourth dimension of church growth. The church will be engaging in mission education and action both locally and around the world .[7] Mims says that missions is the growth measure that puts every other component in its proper perspective. It is the crown of every church's ministry, proof that the teenagers have embraced a biblical worldview.[8] Some things youth administrators can look for would be: an increase in the amount of money given to missions over the last year, an increase in the percentage of youth surrendering to full-time or part-time Christian vocational ministry, an increase in the number of mission projects and participants in mission projects, and an increase in the average number of youth participating in on-going mission education.

The Functions of the Church

In order to determine the most significant principles of church growth, the best place to begin is with the New Testament. If the goal is to establish successful New Testament churches in the 21st Century, it makes sense that the key would be found in Scripture. There are many Scripture passages that deal with church growth and ministry found in various New Testament books. Three of the most significant, however, have to be the Great Commission—Matthew 28:18-20, the Great Commandment—Matthew 22:37-40, and the Great Commitment—Acts 2:42-47. In these three passages of Scripture, five essential functions of the church emerge as clear standards for the development of the New Testament church in every culture and society from New Testament times until Christ returns. That means, regardless of the variables in a community type, ethnic make-up, or financial condition, these five interrelated functions are essential for establishing and holding a kingdom focus and becoming a successful church. The five functions are evangelism, discipleship, fellowship, ministry, and worship.

It makes sense that since youth ministry is a product of the church and a part of the church, successful youth ministry will experience growth as a result of quality execution of these same functions, and thus contribute to the success and impact of the local church. Though others who have studied the purpose of the church may identify these functions by different names, drop, add, or combine a function here or there, most experts agree that these five functions are clearly identified in Scripture. The backbone of this book is built on these five functions. Each chapter will discuss one of the functions and provide suggestions for how youth ministries can address the function in their local church from a youth perspective. The final chapter gives some clear administrative hints that should drive through the functions and enable a youth minister to put together the pieces of the big picture.

The Practice of the Church

Since there is one Great Commission, five biblical functions of a church, and four results of a growing church the question must be asked, how does a church develop a strategy to get from the functions of a church to the results of a church? How does the church, or in this case a youth ministry, help a lost teenager become a Great Commission Christian? What is the process for making disciples, maturing believers in Christ, and helping them to become engaged in multiplying ministry? The answer is found through a close examination of four basic church practice strategies that are a part of a tool known as the Model and Process (MAP). Church practice grows out of the intentional strategy determined by the church and describes the balanced methodologies and essential actions a church, or in this case the youth ministry, a part of the church, employs to engage people in evangelism, discipleship, fellowship, ministry, and worship.

These four church practice strategies are accomplished within a cultural context unique to a local church. This is the context of a church's life that shapes the way it views itself and leads to its unique style and identity. To make disciples, churches will establish open groups and corporate worship opportunities. These serve as entry points into the church for unbelievers. Open group strategies exist to lead teenagers to faith in the Lord Jesus Christ and to build on-mission Christians by engaging the youth in foundational evangelism, discipleship, fellowship, ministry, and worship through on-going evangelistic (small group)

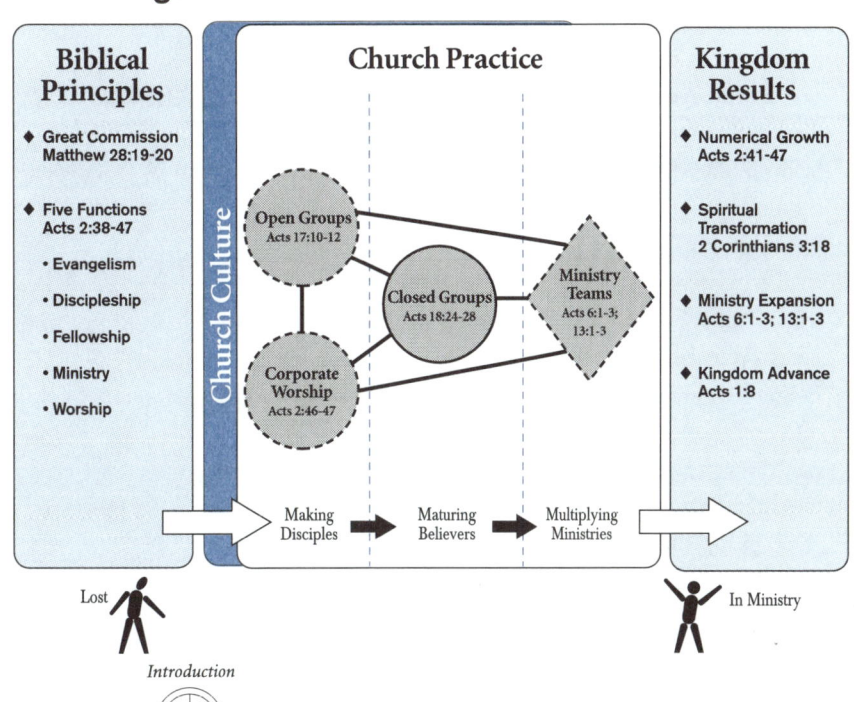

Bible study units of believers together with unbelievers in an atmosphere of compassion to share the gospel.[9] A corporate worship strategy exists for believers to celebrate God's grace and mercy, to proclaim God's truth, and to evangelize the lost in an atmosphere of encountering the presence, holiness, and revelation of Almighty God.[10] Note that the diagram of the MAP includes broken lines representing open groups and corporate worship. This is to indicate these church practice strategies are intended to be open to believers and nonbelievers who often come in and out of these ongoing experiences regularly.

When nonbelievers are saved, they are brought into the fellowship of believers. Mixing with members, new believers come into the body of Christ and begin the journey of following Christ. To help them mature as believers, believers will engage in closed groups to help them discover their gifts for ministry, develop these gifts, find higher accountability, and learn to be a leader. This closed group strategy exists to build kingdom leaders and to equip believers to serve by engaging teenagers in discipleship that moves them toward spiritual transformation through short-term, self-contained training units in an atmosphere of accountability to God and to each other.[11] Note the representation on the diagram for closed groups has an unbroken line indicating these groups are specifically targeted toward believers intent on maturing in their faith. As noted, they are short-term groups with high accountability.

For helping them become multiplying believers, churches will funnel them into ministry teams to give them outlets for ministry and enable them to reproduce themselves in and through others. A ministry team strategy exists to build up the body of Christ to accomplish the work of service within the church and to be involved in missions outside the church through new or existing kingdom units in an atmosphere of prayer and urgency for people in need of God's love.[12] Note the diamond shape of the geometric figure representing ministry teams in the MAP. Ideally these teams minister inward toward the body of believers and outward toward the community. Again, the broken line represents short-term, entry point experiences related to the season of ministry the team ministers within, though much of the equipping for these teams is done within a closed group setting.

Everything done in the youth ministry of a church should fit into one of these four church practice strategies. Each church may draw their MAP a little differently. There may be different sized geometric figures, different kinds of open, closed, or ministry groups with different names for various strategies and programs within their youth ministry, but their goal should be a balance between the different strategies with one strategy not larger than the others. Lost teenagers move into the church through open groups and corporate worship and hopefully become disciples and are assimilated in the church. Then they mature as believers through closed group experiences and as a part of ministry teams. Eventually they become multiplying disciples. Lines connecting the four church practice strategies indicate that all the stages feed, draw support, and connect with one another. The focus of this book is on the five biblical functions of the church (specifically the youth ministry). The idea is to have a balanced ministry based on the five functions (and among the four church practice strategies), which is basic student ministry. Throughout each discussion of a function, however, the authors have identified ways the function can be and often is exercised through the church practice that is a part of the MAP.

Having a strategic vision will help youth ministers develop and manage kingdom-focused youth ministries. Recognizing the biblical functions their church and youth ministry is supposed to accomplish will assist in the planning and implementation of successful ministries. Existing assessments/evaluations focus church leadership teams (including the youth minister) to look at the four strategies and determine effective action plans for implementing the strategy. Learning to evaluate the current condition of youth ministry in a church and fix what may be broken will enable a long tenure of effective ministry to youth in a community. The power of God filtrating through these processes will capture the attention of a lost community and the doors of Hades will not be able to stand against such a force. Experience and education are helpful for the youth minister but it is the power of God through simple biblical strategies executed by effective and prayerful Christian leadership that ensure dynamic results that cannot be explained in human terms—it is basic student ministry in the kingdom-focused church.

[1] Gene Mims, *The Kingdom-Focused Church* (Nashville: Broadman and Holman Publisher, 2003), 89.
[2] Gene Mims, *Kingdom Principles for Church Growth, revised* (Nashville: Life Way Press. 2001), 69-72.
[3] Ibid, 72-80.
[4] Mims, 2003, 91.
[5] Paul Borthwick, *Organizing Youth Youth Ministry* (Grand Rapids: Zondervan Publishing House, 1989), 236-238.
[6] Mims, 2001, 80-84.
[7] Ibid, 84-88.
[8] Mims, 2003, 97.
[9] Mims, 2001, 97.
[10] Ibid.
[11] Ibid.
[12] Ibid.

chapter 1
EVANGELISM

Wesley Black

> *Because God has chosen to redeem people from sin, we must join Him by seeking to evangelize every person in the world.*
> —Gene Mims, Vice President of LifeWay Church Resources

"I DON'T KNOW. WHATEVER. MAYBE. Are there any cute guys there?" Heather had been trying to get Sara to come to Backstage, her youth group's Wednesday night meeting, but was not having much luck.

"Yeah, there's Curt, and Sean, and Josh. You know them and they're real cute. Hey, I went to Blair's party with you last Saturday, so maybe we could go to Backstage tonight and then maybe meet up with someone and get something to drink after it's over tonight?"

"You talk like this Christian stuff is great, but all I see is that it's just stupid rules that nobody cares about." Sara turned to walk to her next class. "I mean, what does it do for you? You go to this Backstage thing and then you go to the parties with me. What difference does it make? Why should I go to Backstage when I can meet cute guys at Blair's house on Saturday night?"

Taylor's conversation with Ashley during lunch that same day took a different turn. Ashley said, "Well, you sure have changed since last summer," between bites of her taco. "I haven't heard any new four-letter words since school started. You used to beat us all in putting someone down with the wildest words. Are you trying out for Miss Prude or something?"

"No," Taylor smiled as she sipped her juice. "I made a commitment to Jesus at summer camp. I guess my whole vocabulary changed. You want to hear about it?"

Unfortunately the realistic situation described above is all too frequent in connection with the youth ministries for which we are responsible. As youth ministers, it is important for us to equip our teenagers to be more like Taylor than Heather. Evangelism is more than telling someone about an event. It is demonstrating the difference Christ makes in our lives and sharing with them how to have a relationship with Christ.

> **Now everything is from God, who reconciled us to Himself through Christ and gave us the ministry of reconciliation: that is, in Christ, God was reconciling the world to Himself, not counting their trespasses against them, and He has committed the message of reconciliation to us (2 Cor. 5:18-19).**

The Greatest Mission Field— Our Own Youth Groups!

Eighty-one percent of the students surveyed consider themselves Christians, yet further questioning revealed that only 32 percent have beliefs that would classify them as born-again Christians. That leaves 49 percent of the teen population who claim to be Christian although they have never come to a saving faith in Jesus Christ! In other words, half of all teenagers are not born again but firmly believe that they are Christians (further referred to as "nominal Christians").

Surprisingly, 31 percent of those nominal Christians are sharing their faith as well, yet do not understand or embrace the true basis of salvation even for their own eternal well-being, let alone the individuals whom they evangelize.

Also some of these nominal Christians—who themselves do not understand the very basis of true faith in Christ— are nearly as numerous as are born-again evangelizers (15% to 20%). So, we have a sizable corps of evangelizers who believe that one gets to heaven either through good works or through God's goodness—not through faith in Christ. In some ways, then, the real task of evangelism is twofold: reaching out with relevance to individuals who are not Christian, but also sensitively challenging and bolstering the

What Is Evangelism?

Evangelism is communicating the good news of Jesus Christ to a nonbeliever with the intent of leading that person to make a life-changing commitment to the lordship of Christ. This involves prayer, verbal conversation, written communication, acts of service, and the example of a lifestyle that brings honor to God.

That's a pretty long definition, so here it is in simple terms. Evangelism is:
- talking to lost people about what God has done in my life
- praying for friends who have not accepted Christ as their Lord and Savior
- chatting with friends online about what God is doing in my life
- taking part in a mission or ministry project
- talking to lost friends about what God can do in their lives
- explaining to someone what the Bible says about becoming a follower of Christ
- living each day so my words and my life both demonstrate my love for and commitment to Christ

No youth ministry can experience success in the absence of evangelism. In fact, almost everything a youth ministry does as a part of a kingdom-focused church should contribute, either directly or indirectly, to evangelism. Unfortunately, many youth ministries claim to be evangelistic or acknowledge the importance of evangelism but really don't do any evangelism. Evangelistic methods are important, but not as important as the message itself—the good news of Jesus Christ. How we present the gospel is important, but not as important as the need to share the gospel.

Jesus and Evangelism?

Jesus was the Master Evangelist as well as the Master Teacher. He showed us several ways to approach evangelism through His earthly ministry. Jesus did not do miracles simply to impress everybody. He didn't even do the miracles to be nice to certain people. After all, there were many people who did not get healed or raised from the dead by Jesus. He performed miracles to reveal Himself and what God is like. Let's take a look at some ways Jesus brought the good news to people through His miracles.

The earthly ministry of Jesus showed that His approach to evangelism was REAL PRAYER.

Relational Evangelism
Environmental Evangelism
Action-oriented Evangelism
Large Group Evangelism
Finally, His earthly ministry was saturated with **Prayer**.

Jesus Shared the Good News Through *Relationships*

Take a look at the first recorded miracle Jesus performed. It's found in John 2:1-11 where He turned the water into wine. Jesus, His disciples, and His mother were at a wedding feast when a catastrophe happened. The refreshments ran low! As a result, Jesus' mother called for Him to do something. Jesus instructed the servants to bring six large containers of

Basic Student Ministry

water. He told the servants to draw out some water and take it to the master. The master tasted the wine (that had just been turned from water into wine) and went to compliment the bridegroom on the fine wine he was now serving at his wedding feast. The master did not know about the miracle, but the servants did.

Because of this miracle, the servants caught a glimpse of who Jesus was, and the disciples put their faith in Him (vv. 9,11). He didn't deliver a sermon or teach a structured lesson. In fact, we do not know if He even said anything about Himself, but the small group around the water pots sure got the message.

This illustrates the principle of working through relationships, especially in social settings. It was a party, not a worship service. It was a gathering of friends enjoying each other's company, and Jesus found a way to reveal Himself without dominating the content of the conversations. Students love to have fun with friends. Christian students also love Jesus and need to find ways to bring their friends into a loving relationship with Him without suddenly getting serious or engaging in heavy discussions about the end times.

Jesus Shared the Good News by Using Words from the *Environment*

In John 3, we meet Nicodemus *(NIK uh DEE muhs)* and first hear the phrase "born again" (v. 3). For whatever reason, Nicodemus came to Jesus at night. John is well known for his use of light as an analogy to belief in Christ. Perhaps John was illustrating that Nicodemus came to Jesus "in the dark" spiritually, not simply after the sun went down.

When Nicodemus showed interest in the kingdom of God, Jesus immediately started talking about the need to be born again. Of course, Nicodemus was puzzled and asked what this was all about. Jesus went on to talk about an earthly birth as compared to a spiritual birth. Jesus knew Nicodemus was a Pharisee. As a Pharisee, Nicodemus placed a lot of value on his family heritage as a Jew. Most Pharisees were devout observers of the law and the traditions of the elders. Jesus said Nicodemus was looking to the wrong family heritage for salvation. He needed to get a new family tree. He needed to be "born again" into the family of God rather than to try to keep the traditions of the Jewish elders.

In the next chapter, Jesus met a very different person from Nicodemus. We find Jesus and His disciples on the way through Samaria, which was not their usual route. (See Matt. 19:1 and Luke 17:11.) Most Jews took a longer route on the other side of the Jordan River to avoid going through Samaria. They looked down on the Samaritans and tried to avoid any contact with them, but Jesus said He "had to go through Samaria" (John 4:4). He had an important witnessing opportunity waiting for Him there.

In the middle of the day, Jesus sat down for a rest and the disciples went into town to buy some food. Jesus began a conversation with a Samaritan woman who was at the well drawing water. This was a shocking thing to those first century Jews. Jesus was a Jew and the woman was a Samaritan, and the two just did not talk to one another. First, she was a woman and He was a man, and it was taboo for people to speak to someone of the opposite sex in public. In addition, He was a spiritual leader and she was an "immoral" woman.

The woman was at the well in the middle of the day, which was highly unusual. Most women came to draw water early in the morning while it was still cool, but they apparently did not want this woman to be part of their crowd. She had been through several failed marriages, and she was living at the time with a man who was not her husband. For this and likely some other reasons, she was forced to come to the well to draw water in the

faith, beliefs, and commitment of nominal Christians.
—Mark Matlock, president WisdomWorks Ministries

This information was taken from the Teens & Evangelism Report, which is based upon research conducted in August 2000 by the Barna Research Group. The research was commissioned by Mark Matlock of WisdomWorks Ministries.

"For God loved the world in this way: He gave His One and Only Son, so that everyone who believes in Him will not perish but have eternal life" (John 3:16).

THE RESPONSIBILITY OF THE CHURCH

It may be that we have one of the most spiritually alive generations, ready to respond to our leadership. With that comes responsibility to train students regarding many of the deeper aspects of the Christian faith. We need to be cautious that we are not misleading students to believe that their religious faith is equivalent to church involvement, but rather that their faith is grounded in a relationship with Christ.

Sixty-six percent of youth group attendees said that their church provides them with opportunities to share their faith, yet only 28 percent had received any training regarding how to share their faith.

The type of faith being disseminated by student evangelizers is a problem—including information from born-again folks. For example, consider the following statistics:

• 23 percent of all evangelizers and 12 percent of born-again evangelizers said the Bible is not accurate in all it teaches.

• 48 percent of evangelizers and 35 percent of born-again evangelizers said the devil, or Satan, is NOT a living being but is a symbol of evil.

• 30 percent of evangelizers and 21 percent of born-again evangelizers believe that when Jesus Christ was on earth He committed sins, like other people.

• 62 percent of evangelizers and 55 percent of born-again

middle of the day when none of the other respectable women were there. So it was a bold move on the part of Jesus to start a conversation with her, but Jesus is often bold in pursuing those who need to hear the good news.

Notice that Jesus started talking about water, even calling it "living water" (John 4:9-10). Later He related that living water to eternal life (v. 14). The woman understood what Jesus was talking about because she tried to change the subject (vv. 19-20) and bring up a religious controversy. Have you ever tried to witness to someone and they tried to get off track by asking some religious trivia question? Jesus made His point—she could have the "living water" He offered and the opportunity to start over with her new life.

Notice that Jesus talked to the Samaritan woman at the well about "living water" while He talked to Nicodemus about being "born again." Why didn't He talk to the woman about being "born again" and to Nicodemus about "living water"? In both cases, Jesus took the words out of the environment and gave them new meaning. Nicodemus was focused on his family heritage and life, so Jesus used the terms that communicated new life to Nicodemus. The language of "living water" would have meant nothing to him. In the same way, the thought of "living water" and never being thirsty again spoke to the woman's deepest needs. Jesus did this on numerous other occasions, as He spoke of seeds, sheep, goats, shepherds, living stones, bread of life, kings, and kingdoms. He had a wonderful ability to take the everyday terms used within a common environment and give them spiritual meaning.

I wonder how Jesus would talk to teenagers today if He met them in the mall, in the hallway at school, on the playing field, or in the car. I suspect He would talk to athletes in terms of game plans, crossing the finish line, endurance, and rules. To the musicians He would talk about the composer, the musical score, living in harmony with others, and watching the director. To the class officer He might talk about running a good campaign, the makeup of the platform, and the winning strategy. In short, He would put the heavenly principles into human terms of the environment to open the door to the kingdom.

Jesus *Actively* Reached out to People

Jesus told a story of a man who planned a great banquet and invited many guests (Luke 14:16-23). When it was time for the banquet to begin, none of the invited guests showed. He then sent out his servants into all the streets and country roads to bring in others. He told his servants to "make them come in, so that my house may be filled" (v. 23). There was a sense of urgency to the request. It was a time for action, not passivity.

There are times when we need to communicate the sense of urgency in our evangelism. Every year high school seniors march across the stage at graduation and are never seen in church again. Some statistics indicate that as many as 87 percent of the teenagers who were once involved at some point in church, drop out and do not participate in the family of faith beyond their high school years. They are literally marching off the stage at graduation into a life apart from the church. That calls for a sense of urgency.

There are any number of outlines of the plan of salvation available today. Tracts and gospel presentations are abundant. Training resources to teach students and adult leaders how to witness are there for the taking. Sometimes we criticize these as "canned approaches" to evangelism. They may seem mechanical and contrived on the surface, like a planned speech that has to be delivered.

When students are trying to explain how to become a Christian, they often grasp for words to describe the simple process of accepting Christ. Teenagers, for all their expanding vocabularies, are not really very good at verbal skills. They sometimes need a helping hand to get a grasp on leading a friend to Christ. Tracts, outlines, illustrations, and other verbal clues can provide the help an adolescent needs to put the gospel into words. (See Appendix 1 for the FAITH gospel presentation.)

Jesus Used Evangelism with *Large Crowds*

Wherever Jesus traveled in His ministry, large crowds soon gathered. As He healed the sick and cast out demons, those around brought their relatives and friends to be healed (Matt. 8:14-16; 15:29-30). When word spread that He was to speak, people came from the whole region to hear Him (Matt. 5:1-2; Mark 2:13; 3:20; 4:1; Luke 8:4; etc.). He used those occasions to reveal Himself and to introduce the people to the kingdom of God.

The people often came to Jesus for selfish reasons. They wanted food or healing. They wanted Him to right the wrongs in their lives. They wanted Him to restore justice or to deal with the oppressive political situation of their day. I doubt there was much close, personal contact between Jesus and the last few guys on the back row at the Sermon on the Mount (Matt. 5-7), but Jesus used the opportunity to address their eternal needs as well as deal with their immediate needs.

Often students attend our youth activities for less than noble reasons. They may be looking for some cheap entertainment or food. They may be there to mix with other teenagers or just to get away from home for a while. We can use opportunities to guide these youth into a saving relationship with Jesus if we will focus on evangelism.

Christian concerts, after-game fellowships, large youth rallies, and youth evangelism conferences are examples of large events that can be used effectively to evangelize students. Distributing tracts or flyers in a neighborhood or a beach reaches out to large numbers of people with the written message. Radio programs, Internet Web sites, e-mail networks, and television spots can reach the masses with the message of Christ's salvation. The emphasis is more on the content of the message than on personal relationships, so this approach must be placed within a balanced approach to evangelism in the overall student ministry strategy.

Prayer Was the Base of Jesus' Evangelism

Jesus was known for many things, but perhaps the most striking was His prayer life. The disciples saw Him speaking, teaching, healing, and confronting. The one thing they specifically requested He teach them about was how to pray (Luke 11:1). Prayer was such an integral part of His life that it saturated everything He did, including evangelism.

Jesus prayed alone and with His disciples on numerous occasions. On the last night the disciples spent with Jesus, He prayed the great prayer recorded in John 17. A remarkable phrase jumps out in verse 20, "I pray not only for these, but also for those who believe in

---

evangelizers contend that there is no such thing as absolute truth; that two people could define truth in different and conflicting ways and both still be correct.

- *89 percent of evangelizers and 83 percent of born-again evangelizers did not even offer a guess as to the meaning of the term "the Great Commission." Only 3 percent of evangelizers and 8 percent of born-again evangelizers offered what could be described as the "right" description of the phrase.*
- *44 percent of evangelizers and 31 percent of born-again evangelizers—and 75 percent of non-Christians—did not offer a guess as to what John 3:16 might refer. Only 26 percent of evangelizers and 37 percent of born-again evangelizers offered a correct description of John 3:16, either reciting the verse or describing the concept of the verse accurately.*

—Mark Matlock, president WisdomWorks Ministries

This information was taken from the Teens & Evangelism Report, which is based upon research conducted in August 2000 by the Barna Research Group. The research was commissioned by Mark Matlock of WisdomWorks Ministries.

Prayer changes not only the circumstances for which you are praying, but also the heart of the one praying. Prayer helps you to overcome feelings of inadequacy, callousness, and selfishness. Change needs to occur in the heart of the one who prays for the unchurched person as much as in the heart of the person being prayed for.
—David Scott, minister to youth, South Main Baptist Church Pasadena, Texas

Me through their message." Jesus was praying for all those who will believe through the disciples' evangelistic efforts and all the believers through the ages. Jesus was praying for us! He was praying for everyone who will come to know Christ through our witnessing.

The bottom line of evangelism is prayer. It is the starting point, the ending point, and all points in between. If Christians are not praying, then all their evangelism plans are simply mechanical efforts to convince someone to believe the way they believe. The heart of evangelism for believers is prayer for lost people.

One answer to getting many reluctant students involved in evangelism is prayer. Youth leaders must teach youth to pray for their lost friends. Emphasize prayer for lost students during all prayer times in Sunday School and other groups at church. Constantly remind them to pray for lost friends in midweek meetings. Lead them to pray as much for lost friends as they do for their sick relatives, for money, or for good grades in school.

During the invitation time at the close of a worship service, when one of those lost teenagers makes a public commitment to Christ, can you guess who will be the first to rush to his or her side with smiles and tears of joy? It will be that timid student who has been praying for his or her salvation. They will have invested their hearts in evangelism through prayer for their lost friends.

EVANGELISM IN YOUR CHURCH

In the Introduction, you have already read about how MAP (Kingdom-Focused Church Model and Process) can be a comprehensive way of looking at the church practice of student ministry in your church. Now let's plug in these church practice strategies to the type of evangelism Jesus used and see how they can be fleshed out in our student ministry groups.

"Go, therefore, and make disciples of all nations, baptizing them in the name of the Father and of the Son and of the Holy Spirit" (Matt. 28:19).

"Repent," Peter said to them, "and be baptized, each of you, in the name of Jesus the Messiah for the forgiveness of your sins, and you will receive the gift of the Holy Spirit." . . . And every day the Lord added those being saved to them (Acts 2:38,47b).

A Kingdom-Focused Church Model and Process

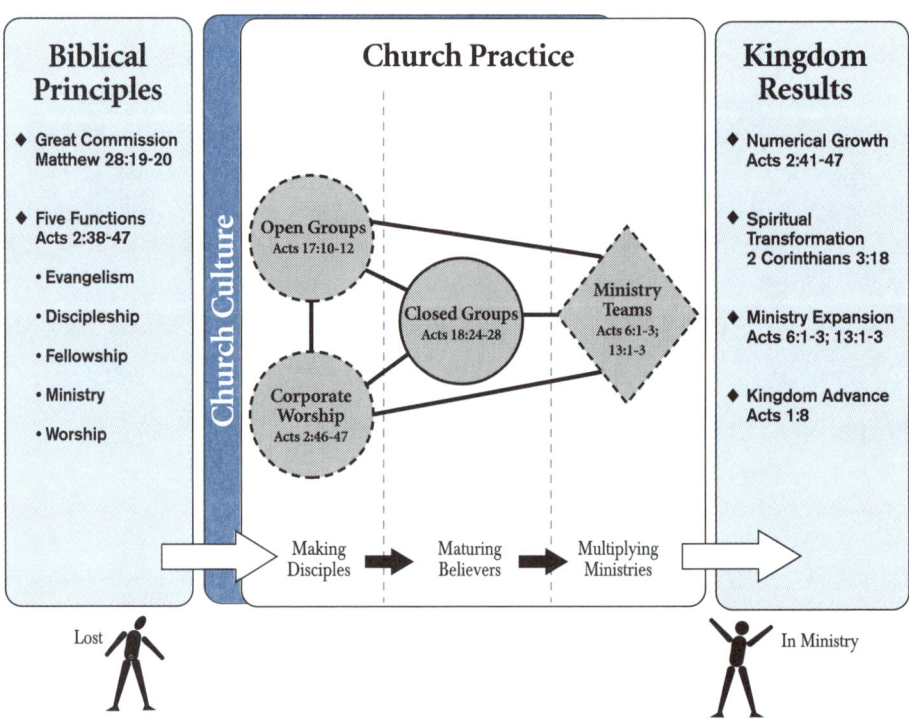

Open Groups

Sunday School classes, ongoing or short-term small group Bible studies, cell groups, affinity groups, and home Bible fellowships are the key ways to establish the foundation of evangelism in any student ministry. Youth can bring their lost friends to small groups for Bible study and fellowship with other believers. During the process of the Bible study, they can hear the good news and be encouraged to invite Christ into their hearts. Follow-up is a natural when youth leaders realize the need to teach for spiritual transformation not just to teach a Bible lesson. These adult leaders and students can help new Christians begin their new lives in Christ and be assimilated into the body of believers.

In most churches, the Sunday School is the open group strategy already in place to function as the major outreach arm of the church. It is a prime avenue for sharing the good news and leading youth to Christ. It takes some thought and attention to shape open groups into vital evangelism links. Most youth ministers would have to admit that although they would like to think their Sunday Schools are evangelistic, careful examination would reveal otherwise.

The definition for *Sunday School* is "the foundational strategy in the local church for leading people to faith in the Lord Jesus Christ and for building on-mission Christians through open Bible study groups that engage people in evangelism, discipleship, ministry, fellowship, and worship." By its very nature, Sunday School or other open small groups are foundational evangelism strategies—meaning that the entire evangelistic youth ministry should be constructed on the strategy of the Sunday School or their other open small groups, whose main purpose is to "lead people to faith in the Lord Jesus Christ."

This means that adult leaders and students need to be aware of the spiritual condition of teens in their groups. As lessons are prepared, as programs are planned, and as activities are conducted, there needs to be a well-constructed, purposeful plan of evangelism in the process. These ministries must target lost teenagers and creatively seek ways to wrap their arms around those who don't yet have a relationship with Christ as a part of the strategy of Sunday School or other open small groups.

Corporate Worship

In my church, like many others, our youth group sits together during Sunday morning worship services. At the invitation time, groups of students kneel at the altar or in a side aisle to pray for lost friends. They understand that the Sunday morning worship time is a key part of the evangelism in our student ministry.

For many students today, the Wednesday night or weekday youth worship meetings are their first point of contact with the church and are another good example of times the gospel plan of salvation can be brought to the surface. Students feel comfortable bringing their friends to this open, inviting time, and they experience the fellowship, worship, prayer, and sense of awe that draws them closer to God. In many churches, the Wednesday evening time is the most student-led program in the youth ministry. This speaks volumes to visitors. They sense this is a church that values teenagers and allows them to have significant leadership roles. Adult small group leaders attend these services and use this opportunity to build relationships with all the students. This makes it easier for new students to come to Sunday School and other open Bible study groups and often opens the door for more evangelistic opportunities.

If teens come to Wednesday nights or Sunday mornings or any other big youth gathering, have a great time, leave with smiles on their faces, but have no sense of an encounter with God, have we really been doing our best for Christ? These are great times to lift up the life-promising claims of the gospel, lead students to make the most important decision they will ever make, then assimilate them back into the ongoing small group Bible study ministry where they can be on mission for Christ.

Camps, retreats, and DiscipleNows are other group worship times that can be seen as evangelistic opportunities. Students should be encouraged to invite their friends, and adult leaders should look for opportunities to build relationships with these new students.

Closed Groups
A balanced student ministry will also include ways for youth to experience more intense study, discipleship, and spiritual growth. Closed groups allow for higher accountability, intense discussions, and learning that builds on prior lessons. Students can be expected to make a more substantial commitment to the group and come prepared for more personal growth. Let's take a look at how evangelism fits in a closed group strategy.

Ongoing (entry level) discipleship groups are great ways to establish foundational beliefs in new Christians. These groups can also equip students to share the gospel in their own words and to develop a prayer strategy for evangelizing their peers. For teenagers who are not yet believers but who happen to attend these entry level discipleship groups, they will be exposed to the gospel presentations during training sessions and have an opportunity to respond to Christ as a result of that exposure.

Accountability groups are great for strengthening discipleship and spiritual growth. As guys or girls meet together in small groups or in pairs, they hold each other accountable in their Christian conduct. How does this impact evangelism? Perhaps the most common complaint of non-Christians is that Christians act no differently than nonbelievers. Christians are seen as impostors who say they believe one way but act another way. This hurts any claim of evangelism that Christ makes a difference in a person's life. Accountability groups encourage Christian students to live lives that model the kind of difference Christ can make.

These accountability groups also hold the participants accountable for actually doing evangelism as well as provide times of encouragement during the process of members sharing Christ with others. Closed Bible study groups that do not lead to or include some form of evangelism, either directly or indirectly, are not real discipleship in the truest sense. True, most discipleship closed groups exist to provide a deeper study of Christian beliefs, attitudes, or skills; these should ultimately result in the expansion of the kingdom of God. A spirit of evangelism should pervade the discipleship process. Otherwise, these closed groups would resemble a team that only met for practice day after day but never engaged in playing the game with another team.

Some musical groups, which are auditioned groups only for Christian teenagers, might be similar to closed discipleship groups. While this "closed" group's purpose may be to prepare intensely for musical performance, the members can also hold each other accountable for spiritual growth through Scripture memory and Bible study. They should also consider the ultimate purpose of their performance as a ministry team, which is more than likely evangelistic or to lead others in worship, and to ultimately build the kingdom of God, not simply to entertain the audience.

Ministry Teams

Ministry teams can grow out of any of the groups already mentioned. They can be long-term groups, or groups that exist only for one event or function. Sunday School leaders or small group Bible study leaders actually are ongoing ministry teams. These leaders should be trained to share the gospel in a variety of ways and know how to lead teenagers to begin their walk with Christ. Let's consider some other possible ministry teams.

Choir or praise and worship bands are strong appeals for many youth who enjoy making music. For many teenagers, sharing their faith through music is the best way they can witness to others. Again, lost teens in choir or the praise and worship bands will be exposed to the gospel through the music they are singing and playing and will have an opportunity to respond. Sports teams on the other hand are the first point of involvement in church for many athletic-minded teens today. They may join things like a church softball or basketball team, a youth bicycle riding group, or a church skating club and begin attending other youth ministry meetings through this involvement. Through the words and influence of a godly coach or club leader and dedicated Christian teammates and fellow athletes, they can come to know Jesus personally as Savior.

A servant evangelism project could be planned and led by a Sunday School group, a discipleship group, a choir, or the entire student ministry team. This is a great way to serve God and share His love through a ministry event. Youth often blitz a neighborhood or beach with tracts, flyers announcing events, or other free materials dealing with the faith. Taking a survey of a neighborhood to determine ministry or evangelism needs is another example of a ministry team in action.

Prayer teams and prayer partners can meet regularly to pray for specific events or for ongoing evangelism. I know many youth in our church who meet at school during lunch or study hall to pray for each other and for lost friends at school. Every major youth function should have a prayer strategy that envelopes the whole thing from beginning to end.

Witnessing teams can go out in small groups of two or three to share the good news with lost students. These often take place during church outreach nights, in preparation for special evangelistic events, and during mission projects. FAITH teams, which ironically are closed groups involved in intense strategic evangelism training, actually become ministry teams when they fan out into the community and do FAITH visits. (For the FAITH outline see Appendix 1.)

A lead team (see chapter 6) can be in charge of planning all evangelism events for a student ministry. This team can plan major events for the whole student ministry or can coordinate with the ongoing Sunday School strategy of outreach and witnessing.

Tips for Evangelistic Church Practice Strategies

Here are some suggestions to help make open groups, closed groups, worship experiences, and ministry teams more evangelistic:

1. Have Youth Sunday School leaders present and involved on Wednesday night. This is a great relationship-building time. Adults who spend time visiting and getting to know the students, especially the visitors, will have a wide open door to get those students involved in Sunday morning Bible study times.
2. Have a heavy dose of student leadership on Wednesday nights. Students should be the ones leading music and worship, leading games and skits, sharing testimonies, reading Scripture passages, leading prayers, making announcements, operating sound and audiovisual equipment, and welcoming everyone. In many churches, the youth are in

---

Bob Dietz has been teaching seventh graders in Sunday School for a number of years at First Baptist Church in Richardson, Texas. Every year he begins the Sunday School year with about 10 youth on his Sunday School roll. By the end of each year, it always seems his enrollment more than doubles. He visits his class members and prospects, and he also uses the telephone very effectively. Through his use of the telephone, visitation, and notes, Bob is practicing an evangelistic approach that used to be called Continual Contact Consciousness (CCC). His class members and prospects know by his regular, consistent contacts that Bob cares about them. Through this strategy, he communicates care and concern. Youth leaders can practice similar strategies through telephone calls, notes of encouragement, and personal visits.

charge of leading the entire program.

3. Offer an invitation to accept Christ. Sometimes this will mean having an invitation to come forward and publicly profess Christ. At other times, this might mean filling in a commitment card to get more information. Use variety and creativity, but make time for life-changing decisions.

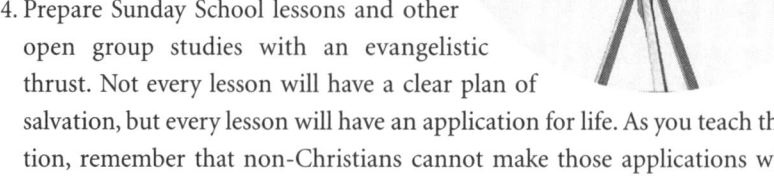

4. Prepare Sunday School lessons and other open group studies with an evangelistic thrust. Not every lesson will have a clear plan of salvation, but every lesson will have an application for life. As you teach the application, remember that non-Christians cannot make those applications without the Holy Spirit guiding their lives. Find creative ways to share about the change Christ can make in a person's life.

5. Emphasize the urgency for evangelism and hold students accountable for their witness in closed group experiences. Students must be equipped efficiently and then challenged to share their faith with others, knowing someone will not only be praying for them as they witness but holding them accountable for their witness.

6. Enlist students regularly to share a brief testimony. Help them learn how to put it into words clearly. Give them an outline and lead them to practice telling it to you. Be sure they include some word about how God is moving in their lives today.

7. Make purposeful efforts to have non-Christians present, or, as a result of the strategy, specifically engage lost teenagers in the ministry. You cannot expect evangelistic results unless you have non-Christians to hear the gospel. Never settle for having only the same kids present every time. There is a lost world that needs to hear the gospel, and we are the ones who must communicate to them.

8. Ensure that ministry teams are not only meeting needs and offering student ministry leadership, but that they are meeting needs in the name of Christ and leading with an eye on the gospel.

EVANGELISM STRATEGIES

Before we launch into how to do evangelism, we need to ask ourselves an important question: Is evangelism an event or program, or is it a lifestyle? I'm afraid we send subtle messages to youth that evangelism is an isolated event, or it's something only special Christians do. It should be the ordinary, normal thing that run-of-the-mill Christians do. You don't have to have special training to evangelize. You don't have to be certified or know how to use a certain tract or outline to be able to witness. You don't have to have a position or title in the church to witness. Too often we treat evangelism as something we do instead of a lifestyle. We schedule evangelism events, conferences, or activities. We plan a time for outreach on the calendar. When the evangelism event, schedule, or activity is finished, we go back to business as usual until the next time we *do evangelism*.

Jim Burns says that, "too many of us spin our wheels when it comes to evangelism. As we've evaluated our own outreach programs, we've seen that we often wasted time, effort, and money on activities that didn't accomplish the goal of reaching unchurched students in our community. Instead, we developed evangelistic meetings for Christians."[2]

How sad that we have relegated evangelism to a small corner of our Christian life. It's so easy to ignore it or get too busy doing other religious things and simply forget to live an evangelistic lifestyle. As we talk about evangelism strategies and events, I pray we never forget evangelism is a lifestyle, a way we approach every day and every relationship.

Campus Evangelism Strategies

Where do students spend most of their waking hours? Where do students spend the most time with their peers? Chad Childress says:

> Do you know where over 95 percent of all youth can be found seven hours a day, five days a week, nine months out of the year for seven years of their lives? And no, it is not their beds. It is their school campuses. Youth may not be excited about it, but it is where they spend most of their time. If the campus is where youth are, then it is up to us to seek to make an impact on the campus. We must go where they are.[3]

Campus Christian Clubs.—Some of the most exciting evangelism happening today is based in campus Christian clubs. The concept is catching on all across America because of a common desire among many Great Commission Christians to reach students for Christ. Challenge 2000 Alliance is made up of various denominations and parachurch groups that have committed to reaching the 56,000 secondary schools in America through Great Commission clubs on the school campuses. These clubs are designed to meet the challenge in two ways: (1) to commission students to be campus missionaries to their school campuses, and (2) to challenge student ministers and other youth leaders to support the campus missionaries.[4]

Congress passed the Equal Access Act in response to restrictions by some schools and courts that discriminated against religious speech and voluntary religious meetings by students on school campuses. Public schools have times when noncurriculum-related student groups meet outside of class time. This is known as "limited open forum," which allows students to join various student groups or clubs on school premises. If groups such as the chess club and the scuba club are allowed to meet, the Equal Access Act states the school must also allow students who wish to meet for religious purposes to do so.[5]

Youth ministers and other adult leaders often meet students on campus for fellowship and encouragement. There is no legal right that ensures adults have free access to school campuses. Court decisions recognize that "public school officials have an interest in maintaining discipline and avoiding a disruption of the educational process. Therefore, no citizens have an unqualified right to enter the public high school campus without the permission of school officials."[6] Students have the right to share their religious beliefs as long as they do not interrupt classes and it is done in a volunteer setting.

Campus Christian clubs give Christian students the potential to reach their friends at school and incorporate them into their churches. They are not just Bible clubs, religious study groups, or prayer groups. They are a strategy for accountability and encouragement, outreach, and follow-up. The best approach has proven to be a team approach–youth ministers and youth leaders, students, Christian faculty members, and church members. The youth leaders provide the training and encouragement, the students initiate and carry out the work of the clubs, Christian faculty members act as sponsors on the campus, and the church members provide prayer and financial support.

"Follow me," He told them, "and I will make you fishers of men!" (Matt. 4:19).

One of the most successful approaches is the FiSH strategy for campus clubs. This is based around a four-week rotating schedule of meetings. These four weeks are based on the acronym FiSH and then follow-up. For more information on this strategy check out the student North American Mission Board Web site, *www.studentz.com/fish*.

Campus Christian clubs are not the magic cure for reaching school campuses. Some clubs lose their edge when they run into problems such as the following:

- They become Christian social clubs, providing only fellowship and socializing for Christian students
- They become a place for theological debate over points of doctrine and theology
- They become a "holy huddle" for Christians
- They become simply another Bible study
- They become an end in themselves and lose the connection with the local churches
- They forget that the main purpose is to reach out to non-Christians and bring them to Christ

There is a helpful Web site at *http://youthworkers.net/Pulse*, which provides a way to check the health of campus clubs. The measuring instrument asks three questions in five main areas to gauge the health and vitality of the club. These five areas form the acronym PULSE. To evaluate the health of your campus club, ask yourself these questions to check your PULSE:

Prayer—pursue an active prayer strategy
- Are a growing number of students praying consistently?
- Are individuals and groups at the school being prayed for by name?
- Are prayer needs and results being shared with others?

Unity—in heart, mind, and purpose on campus
- Is communication taking place between various Christian groups?
- Is there a shared vision for reaching students?
- Are relationships of trust being built?

Leadership—engage in student-led, adult-supported ministry
- Are students and adults developing their God-given skills and modeling Christlike living?
- Are adults mentoring and discipling students?
- Are students reaching students on and off campus?

Sharing—exercise an active plan to communicate the gospel to every student
- Is there a vision and burden for reaching those without Christ?
- Are multiple strategies being utilized?
- Are students and adults taking time to build relationships with those who do not know Christ?

Equipping—receive ongoing training to reach students for Christ
- Are students and adults involved in purposeful and effective training?
- Are relevant topics and felt needs being addressed?
- Is there an atmosphere of encouragement and celebration about what God has done?

Student Ministers and Campus Ministry.—Student ministers today recognize the value and necessity of reaching out to students where they spend most of their waking hours. This means visiting with students and building relationships on school campuses. We have already pointed out that legally we cannot force our rights to be on the school campuses, but that does not mean we cannot have a presence there. It all depends on how you go about it. It is important to begin to establish a relationship with the principal, vice-principal, and other key leaders before any on-campus strategy is initiated. Help the principal understand your concern for students and your desire to help support the school. Be honest, but don't be arrogant. Be confident and don't be intimidated by the principal. The important thing is to build a positive relationship that can be strengthened in the future.

While many student ministers meet with students during lunch, this may not be the best time to spend on campus. If it is open and you are free to do so, go for it. Principals often have to deal with many problems and you may look like just another "loose cannon." If so, the principal may not appreciate your presence on campus and may actually forbid you to be there during class times. If this is the case, find ways to meet with students off campus or at times other than class time on campus.

Take a look at the apostle Paul and how he approached his visit to the Areopagus in Acts 17:16-34. Using this model, let's look at how to approach the open door to the campus:

1. Detail the school.—Make a detailed observation of the situation. Paul said, "I see that you are extremely religious in every respect. For as I was passing through…" (vv. 22-23). In the same way you can take a "walking tour" of the school to observe the situation.
2. Attend school events.—Most all school events are open to the public.
   a. Decide what events to attend.—Consider athletic and nonathletic events.
   b. Obtain the events schedule.—Call the school office and ask for a schedule of events. Ask for ways you can support the school as a member of the community.
   c. Fill in your calendar.—Put as many of the events on your calendar as possible.
   d. Observe the school.—Go to the event the majority of the school will attend. Arrive early and stay late. Be observant of youth and adults, how they relate, how they respond, and the overall tone of the community.
   e. Make a journal of what you see.—Write down observations and names of people you meet.
3. Study the school yearbook.—Make the same type observations as you did at the school events. You can usually get a yearbook from last year or borrow one from a student.
4. Subscribe to the school newspaper.—You can get a good feel for what the students are thinking about.
5. Interview students.—Set up an appointment with four to eight students to get a better idea of what's in or out, where most students hang out, who the popular students are, what activities students participate in, and so forth.
6. Interview teachers.—Ask similar questions. This will also give insight into the administration of the school.
7. Visit the hangouts.—Overcome your hesitation and go to where kids hang out. Don't intrude into private parties, but go to public places, especially the popular hangouts after the games.
8. Define their basic motivations.—Each school will have a few basic motivations like athletics, drugs, parties, academics, and so forth.
9. Serve a need.—Discover needs the school has and find a way to meet these needs. It might be chaperons for events, transportation for equipment, or substitute teachers.[8]

Evangelism Strategies with Parents

Among the attributes of today's student ministry is the growing realization of the importance of parents in the lives of students. I once had a student we'll call Josh (not his real name), who was the "thorn in my flesh." He had the attention span of a flea, was loud and obnoxious, and loved to be the one who stirred up the group with controversial topics. I went to visit him at his home and was greeted by his mother, a sweet, gentle soul. My first thought was, *When did you adopt Josh?* because I could not imagine this being her natural son. Then Josh's dad came into the room and we began to talk. It soon became apparent the dad was loud, rambunctious, and loved to stir up controversy. Then I thought, *So this is where Josh gets it! He really is his father's son.*

Our students are like their parents in many ways. Even the most dedicated Christian students from nonbelieving homes have traits, personalities, temperaments, and mannerisms that reflect their parents' influence. I often ask student leaders about the percentages of youth who attend their churches without their parents. The percentages are often staggeringly high. One of the perennial concerns is how to reach out to non-Christian parents.

Reaching Non-Christian Parents.—I wish I could list the top ten wonder-working ideas for reaching out to non-Christian parents and bringing them into the kingdom. There's no doubt about it—it's hard work and will take a lot of effort, but the effort is worth the benefit. A student who is in a Christian home stands a much better chance of avoiding many adolescent risks and remaining faithful to the church long after high school graduation.

Here are a few ideas for reaching non-Christian parents that have proven helpful in my years of youth ministry:

1. Collect family information from teens. Get students to fill in information slips when they visit your activities. Be sure to get essential information like parents' names, mailing address, home telephone number, e-mail address, and other family members, like siblings.
2. Pass along this information to Adult Sunday School classes so they can establish contact with the parents.
3. Pass along this information to teachers of youth from these homes. Enlist the teachers to pray for these parents and find ways to make contact with them on a regular basis.
4. Put all the parents of teenagers on a mailing list to send information about youth events. Use the correct names of the parents. Don't assume that parents and teenagers have the same last names. Send a regular newsletter just for parents, with news and updates on upcoming and long-range youth activities.
5. Visit in the homes of non-Christian parents and build relationships with them. If these parents do not know you, they may become suspect of all the good things their

teenagers are saying about "those adults down at the church." One of the favorite punishments of non-Christian parents is to ground their teenagers from church activities. There is less chance of this happening if the parents know you personally and believe that you are trying to partner with them.

6. Enlist non-Christian parents to host a fellowship in their home. If they have a swimming pool, a backyard barbecue, or a lake home, they will often be willing to have teenagers in for a fellowship time. Enlist enough adult sponsors to provide all the food and cover kitchen duties. This will give quality time between the adults and provide ways to build relationships with the non-Christian parents. You will be surprised how much easier it is for the non-Christian parents to get involved when they have already established relationships with other adults at the church.

7. Send out parenting tips on a regular basis. Use publications such as *Living with Teenagers* as outreach materials. Collect ideas from magazines and books and send these along to parents on a regular basis. Some Sunday School curriculum may have parent newsletters built into the format of the resource.

8. Send out help in understanding teenage culture to parents. Keep them informed about movies, television shows, music, video games, and Internet sites that can be positive or negative influences on their teens.

9. Invite non-Christian parents to all parenting conferences, seminars, and discussions you conduct. Enlist Christian parents to make personal contact and offer to bring them along to the meetings. These can be great sources of ministry to parents, as well as opportunities to share the good news.

Parent Classes for Non-Christian Parents.—Raising teenagers ranks among the most difficult jobs ever faced by human beings. Solving the world's financial problems, understanding Einstein's Laws of Relativity, and filling out your tax returns pale in comparison to understanding the thinking and behavior of a teenager. Most parents and teenagers somehow survive the years, but most parents wonder how they will ever make it while in the middle of parenting in the adolescent years.

Most parents of teenagers are open to any help they can get for handling the daily trials and challenges of adolescence. This includes non-Christian parents of students in your youth group. This can be an open door to building relationships and bringing the gospel to these people.

Event-type Evangelism

Let's face it, teenagers love events. They love to be with crowds of other teenagers. One of the stereotypes of youth ministry through the years is that we only live from one event to another. It's true that youth ministry is much more than events, especially large events. These can also be some key evangelism opportunities if these events are part of an overall, well-balanced strategy of evangelism in student ministry. One of the keys to anchoring these events into the overall youth ministry evangelistic strategy is to assimilate the lost teenagers and new youth believers who participate in these events into the Sunday School or ongoing small group Bible study ministry.

Summer Camp, Retreats, and DiscipleNow.—Summer youth camp is a longtime favorite in youth ministry. Countless numbers of teenagers have come to know Jesus as Savior through the experience of summer camp. Many others have grown deeper in their faith or answered a call to vocational ministry during a youth summer camp. Retreats and DiscipleNow weekends have often had similar results. These days of concentrated time apart from the normal, everyday routines provide the opportunity to focus on God and the promises of the gospel.

Sadly, some summer camps and retreats do not provide the opportunity to share the message of salvation. The programs may be filled with fellowship times, recreation, unhealthy food, lack of sleep, and pranks. They may even have Bible studies and discipleship studies for Christians and still ignore the invitation to repent and follow Jesus. While there may be a place for all these (even bad camp food) in youth ministry, it would be sad to pass up the opportunity for teenagers to change their eternal destinations.

All the elements that make up a camp or retreat can be flavored with an evangelistic appeal. DiscipleNow weekends can be great avenues for a teenager to accept Christ. (DiscipleNow weekends are intense weekends of study, worship, discipleship, ministry, and fellowship, normally held in church members' homes.) Some of these events may be designed primarily for discipleship and training of Christians, but even with that emphasis, there can be times of prayer for lost friends and revival.

Here are some tips and suggestions for building evangelism into your retreats, DiscipleNow weekends, and summer camp.

1. Make it easy for lost teenagers to attend. They cannot sign up and attend if they do not know about it. Keep a mailing list of prospects and make sure they all get flyers and brochures for scheduled events. Offer special deals for nonchurch kids to attend.
2. Offer incentives for youth group members to invite non-Christian friends. Some churches will allow non-Christian teens to attend some events free or for a reduced fee. Others will allow the members to attend free if they recruit a certain number of non-Christian friends to attend at the reduced fee. You will need to budget for this in your youth ministry budget, or recruit donations to cover these expenses.
3. Plan for a direct evangelistic invitation during some part of the program. This doesn't have to be during a large-group worship service. Small groups can have a sharing time when members can talk about Jesus or how they came to be Christians.
4. Offer a public invitation time early in the program of camps and retreats. Sometimes the invitation is delayed until the last night of camp or the closing part of the retreat, as a "highlight" of the program. If the invitation is offered earlier in the program, there will be time for better counseling, follow-up, and basic discipleship for the new Christian during the rest of the time of the camp or retreat.
5. Equip adult leaders to witness to youth. Before the camp or retreat, conduct a training session and give the adult leaders the materials and encouragement to witness to youth in their groups. For an example of the FAITH outline see Appendix 1.
6. Equip students to be bold witnesses. Part of the preparation for any camp or retreat should be providing students with the vision of witnessing to their friends.
7. Hold intentional prayer times for lost students who attend the events. Meet with adult leaders every day during a summer camp to pray for lost students. Provide a sharing time for leaders to talk about significant decisions made during Bible studies and devotionals they lead. Make adults responsible for a small group during the event and encourage them to pray for these students by name.
8. Keep track of everyone who attends the event. Following every camp, retreat, or DiscipleNow weekend, collect the information from registration slips that will help in future evangelism efforts.

Christian Concerts.—Teenagers are drawn to music, and therefore it makes a great evangelistic tool. I had a friend during my seminary days who had a personal ministry taking students to Christian concerts. He was not on a church staff, but was a volunteer youth leader in his church. He loved to attend concerts and often bought tickets and invited teens to attend with him. He always found ways to invite non-Christian students to attend the concerts. He would describe how the Christian bands sounded like mainstream popular bands to get the interest and attention of the non-Christian teens. Following the concerts, he would find ways to lead the other Christian students to share their faith with the non-Christian students as they talked about the music and the band. Many teens came to know the Lord through this ministry.

Churches today often host Christian bands for a concert. While this may be limited to larger churches, many smaller churches can attend and support the concerts. Associational groups can join together and host a Christian concert at a school auditorium or a larger church facility. Youth ministries in a community can band together to sponsor a Christian concert and use the opportunity to invite non-Christian students.

In our city we have planned citywide youth ministry events that involve youth and adults from a variety of evangelical groups. By working together, we could reach many students that might not be interested if the event were held in a church. By having the concert in the school auditorium, we could reach out to many non-Christian teens.

Servant Evangelism.—We have often done ministry projects in our community that had wonderful evangelistic results. Youth love to serve if they sense the project is for a worthy cause and deserving of their time and effort. They will work long, hard hours for the cause of Christ if we give them the opportunity. While this list is not exhaustive, here are a few examples of servant evangelism that youth groups have used:

- Door-to-door survey. Create a simple questionnaire and assign youth to a designated section of residential blocks. They don't have to do the evangelism during the survey time, but they should be equipped to respond if someone expresses interest in knowing more.
- Door-to-door invitations to special events. Distribute free materials and invite the community to attend an event at the church, such as a Fourth of July celebration, fall festival, and so forth.
- Free car wash. People usually expect to pay a donation. In this case, use it as a time to provide a ministry following a rainy season. Hand out brochures about your church after washing the cars.
- Free house repair. Offer to repair a roof or fallen-down porch or steps for people who may not be able to afford the repairs. If this is done without expectation for payment, it can carry a strong message of the love of Christ in a tangible way for the neighborhood.
- Random acts of kindness. Helping people in a time of need carries a message of hope and love to people in a world that often seems cold and insensitive. Instead of receiving payment, just speak a good word for Jesus.
- Hosting a carnival or block party. These can be wonderful times of sharing with people who normally would not associate with Christians. Look for informal ways to share a good word about what Christ can bring to a person's life.

Youth Rallies.—Students usually look for something to do following a big football game or school event. An after-game fellowship provides the place for youth to enjoy wholesome fun and meet other Christian friends. We have often conducted a fellowship time

If you want teenagers to reach other teenagers, they must first see leaders reach teenagers. It is a healthy habit to involve teenagers in your outreach-evangelism efforts. Taking teenagers with you when making visits gives you time to build relationships with class members. When visiting with teenagers, give them a part to play within the visitation process. When visiting prospects who are already Christians, have the teenager visiting with you tell the prospect about specific events and activities going on with your class. When visiting a non-Christian, have the teenagers visiting with you pray for you and the non-Christian during the gospel presentation. Taking teenagers with you during visits is a real plus.
—David Scott, minister to youth, South Main Baptist Church, Pasadena, Texas.

"But you will receive power when the Holy Spirit has come upon you, and you will be My witnesses in Jerusalem in all Judea and Samaria, and to the ends of the earth" (Acts 1:8).

with other church youth groups after games, contests, and festivals. The program can involve music, skits, videos of the game, and crazy contests. It should also include a time of testimony or a brief message of Christ's love.

Use creative ways to gather information about decisions at these rallies. Instead of having a public invitation and asking people to come forward and stand at the front, try placing a card on each chair and telling people to indicate their interest in knowing more.

Many associations and communities will also have youth rallies on weekday nights or weekends. These can be during special seasons (beginning or end of school), during holidays (New Year's Eve, Fourth of July), or as part of a citywide youth emphasis. An important element of these rallies should always be a time of commitment, a time for training for evangelism, or prayer for lost teenagers. Worship times during these youth rallies can be powerful times of prayer for revival. Teens today are hungry for intense times of worship and concentration. Evangelism should naturally grow out of these experiences.

PRAYER STRATEGIES

Too often we think of prayer like we think of a zipper—we open and close everything with it! We should think of prayer as the beginning and ending of everything we do, especially in our evangelism strategies.

An Overall Prayer Strategy

Every event planned in youth ministry should be saturated with prayer. This means more than just praying before our planning meetings. It means more than praying for God to bless our efforts. It even means more than just praying often for the success of the event.

Every element of youth ministry should grow out of the purposeful, intense seeking of the movement of God, and then joining God in that work. We must pray first for God to reveal how He is moving, what He intends to happen, what would bring glory to Him, and what would enlarge His kingdom. Then, and only then, we should begin to build youth ministry plans to join Him in that work. That is the work of prayer.

One of the major elements of any youth event is the undergirding prayer strategy. Some of the elements of a prayer strategy, especially for major events, are:

- A prayer calendar leading up to the event. Write detailed prayer suggestions for all the preparations at least a month ahead of the event.
- A prayer list. Make a list of everyone involved in the planning, everyone who will be leading, all the workers involved, and all the students who will be attending. Share this with the youth, their parents, and with Adult Sunday School classes, and invite them to pray continually for these persons.
- Make prayer reminders. Many groups use hospital armbands, dog tags, or bookmarks as prayer reminders. Church members can be matched with prayer partners.
- Pray specifically for lost teenagers who will be involved in the event. Begin a list of prospects and pray for them often.
- Hold a prayer vigil. Plan a 24-hour prayer vigil the day before the beginning of the event. Challenge youth and adults to sign up for a time slot to pray for the event and lost teenagers. Establish a prayer chain so people can call the next person on the prayer chain to remind them to pray.
- Pray continually during the event. Many churches will have round-the-clock prayer schedules for a summer camp or mission trip. Many adults will volunteer to pray at specified times for lost people to come to know the Lord during the event.

Basic Student Ministry

Prayer Walks

One of the most popular prayer strategies is prayer walking. This is on-the-spot prayer for a place, for an event, or for lost persons in the location where you are prayer walking. Individuals or small groups can walk through a location and pray as they observe people along the way. This is especially helpful with an advance team preparing for a youth mission trip.

EQUIPPING STUDENTS FOR EVANGELISM

We are called to make disciples, not just converts. This means our job as youth leaders is not to do all the evangelism, but to equip the saints to do the work of ministry (Eph. 4:11-12). Some youth leaders are wonderful communicators and evangelists. We must be more than "youth evangelists"; to be faithful to God's Word, we are to be equippers also.

First, this starts with all our Bible study and discipleship efforts. Today we have to deal with many worldview questions that ultimately affect all evangelism. Is Jesus the only way to get into heaven? Who says Christians are right and non-Christians are wrong? How do we know? Can't there be more than one truth? If a person doesn't accept Christ, are they really going to hell? Isn't that awfully narrow thinking?

These are real questions facing teens in today's world. We must equip adult leaders to address these in realistic ways as we teach Sunday School, guide discipleship groups, and lead small groups in camps and retreats.

Second, we should offer more than one way for our students to be involved in evangelism. Jesus approached evangelism in several ways, ranging from highly relationship-oriented to highly content-oriented. Some students may respond well to a memorized outline of the gospel. Others will be able to handle a tract or a testimony in witnessing. Still others will participate best simply by praying for their lost friends. Schedule training sessions at various times during the year to keep students equipped for an evangelistic lifestyle. During training times for mission trips, always include a variety of ways for students to learn to share the gospel. Even during Bible studies, provide simple ways to share the plan of salvation or a testimony. (See the FAITH outline in Appendix 1.)

Third, plan for times of sharing following camps, mission trips, retreats, revivals, and DiscipleNow weekends. Call for youth who have made decisions to tell about their commitments. Also, call on those who invited friends or who shared a testimony with a friend that led to a decision for Christ.

Fourth, keep track of where teenagers make decisions for Christ. Not everyone makes a public decision for Christ during Sunday morning worship services. Some will make that commitment during Wednesday night youth services, some during summer camp, some at a retreat, and others during a DiscipleNow weekend. Some will make a decision during a campus Christian club meeting at school. Still others will pray to receive Christ during a visit in their homes. Don't neglect these opportunities. Look for a variety of opportunities for people to be saved.

Finally, don't neglect the essential elements of follow-up for new Christians. As soon as possible lead them to participate in a baptismal experience. This initial step of obedience is often overlooked or low on the priority list for most new believers. It will help in confirming their decision to follow Christ. Also, provide them with written materials to help them understand their decision. Match them up with a student or adult to meet one-on-one, or provide a new Christian class to help them begin their spiritual journey. The days following a new commitment for Christ are extremely important. New Christians can be powerful influences on their old circles of non-Christian friends.

Evangelism

I am haunted by the story of Mitchell Johnson, who was active for awhile in his church youth group, but ended up gunning down his fellow students at Westside Middle School in Jonesboro, Arkansas. Veteran youth pastor Chris Perry said, "Mitchell spent about six weeks in my ministry and had professed his faith in Christ during a youth revival at my church. I saw the fear and confusion in his eyes, and I remember the outrage I felt. This memory hurts. Could I have done something differently with him?"[9]

I can' help but wonder about that student's relationship with the Lord. I wonder if any one of his friends ever confronted him with the real hope for new life that Jesus offers? I wonder if he represents many teens today who simply take part in church, just so they can hang out with other teenagers? I wonder how seldom we challenge our teenagers to live boldly for Christ?

LEADING AN EVANGELISTIC YOUTH MINISTRY

Erwin McManus said, "America's best atheists are children of the church."[10] The church has had a diminishing influence on society in general, and our children in particular. They are turning away from it in large numbers, but we can still do something about it.

Teens are hungry for significant challenges in their lives. The very nature of adolescence cries for a challenge. George Gallup says of America's "millennials" (persons 19 and younger), "What the churches today do or do not do in seeking to reach our nation's youngest members will have long-term implications in terms of giving young people spiritual moorings for the societal challenges ahead. This is an opportunity that must not be missed."[11]

They live in a world of ideals and hunger for a chance to do something significant. There is an urgency about evangelism. There is no plan B for eternal life. What more significant thing can a person do than help a friend change their eternal destination? Beyond that, as Gene Mims has said, "We are God's plan for evangelizing the world. He has no other. We are His plan, and our obedience means growth in the kingdom and in the churches where we worship and serve."[12]

A study of the New Testament reveals this startling discovery: The New Testament words for *witness* and *martyr* are the same! Christians in the first century knew that sharing their "witness" was the same as putting their lives on the line. How often have we tried to make evangelism easy? Perhaps evangelism is the life challenge that many students are searching for and we should proudly hold that challenge up to them.

If our students respond to that challenge, then this could be the generation that completes the task of reaching the whole world with the gospel.

---

[1]Adapted from Dean Finley, *Handbook for Youth Evangelism,* Nashville: Broadman Press, 1988, 9-11.
[2]Jim Burns and Mike DeVries, *The Youth Builder,* Ventura: Gospel Light, 2001, 87.
[3]Chad Childress, "Winning Youth Through Campus Missionaries," in Richard Ross and Len Taylor, *Leading an Evangelistic Youth Ministry,* Nashville: LifeWay Press, 1999, 89.
[4]Ibid., p. 88.
[5]Marshall Albritton, "Legal Aspects of the Campus," chapter 12 in Barry St. Clair and Keith Naylor, *Penetrating the Campus,* Wheaton, IL, Victor Books, 1993, 189-90.
[6]Ibid., p. 191.
[7]Accessed from Internet Web site *http://www.catchthis.net/strategy.htm.*
[8]Barry St. Clair and Keith Naylor, *Penetrating the Campus,* Wheaton: Victor Books, 1993, 55-62.
[9]Chris Perry, "The Calling," *Group,* September/October 1999, 71.
[10]Erwin Raphael McManus, *An Unstoppable Force: Daring to Become the Church God Had in Mind,* Loveland: Group, 2001, 28.
[11]George Gallup and D. Michael Lindsay, *The Gallup Guide: Reality Check for 21st Century Churches,* Loveland: Group, 2002, 15.
[12]Gene Mims, *Kingdom Principles for Church Growth,* LifeWay Press: Nashville, TN, 2001, 39.

chapter 2
DISCIPLESHIP

Karen Jones

> *Discipleship is simply the practice of realizing the presence of God in our lives. We cannot only talk with God and ask Him life questions—we can live in Him! The ability to shape lives only comes from Jesus. He offers it to us freely (Titus 3:3-8). Discipleship is only realized in the power of God, yet it is easy (Matt. 11:28-29); easy when we place our lives in the mercy of God. There are no shortcuts—maturity takes time.*

"I WILL ALWAYS REMEMBER THE SUMMER of my senior year in high school. I worked with a World Changers mission team in a Muslim country. For the first time in my life, my eyes were opened to a world that existed outside of mine. I saw people in need. I saw a world hurting, a world with no direction or meaning. I met and talked with the very missionaries that I support with my missions offering. Above all, I learned that there is a world out there that does not know the love and forgiveness of Christ, and most of us simply sit at home with that knowledge and do nothing with it. My mission experience instilled in me a need to actively share with others the love that Christ has for us, and the hope that we truly have."

—*Nick, 22*
Oklahoma City, Oklahoma

Nick's overseas mission experience was a watershed experience for him. By acting on the discipleship principles he had committed to intellectually, he was transformed affectively. His beliefs were internalized and solidified. Nick is now in college, majoring in broadcasting. As a result of his deeper commitment to the priorities of Christ and obedience to Him, Nick has spent the last two summers working with North American Mission Board projects in the United States. He will fulfill a portion of his college internship requirement by working alongside a representative of the International Mission Board, a man he met on the field during that life-changing trip to a Muslim country. Personal spiritual disciplines are an important part of his daily life, and he currently volunteers as a youth leader in his local church.

> Then Jesus came near and said to them, "All authority has been given to Me in heaven and on earth. Go, therefore, and make disciples of all nations, baptizing them in the name of the Father and of the Son and of the Holy Spirit, teaching them to observe everything I have commanded you. And remember, I am with you always, to the end of the age" (Matt. 28:19-20).

> When I came to you, brothers, announcing the testimony of God to you, I did not come with brilliance of speech or wisdom. For I determined to know nothing among you except Jesus Christ and Him crucified. And I was with you in weakness, in fear, and in much trembling. My speech and my proclamation were not with persuasive words of wisdom, but with a demonstration of the Spirit and power, so that your faith might not be based on men's wisdom but on God's power (1 Cor. 2:1-5).

> I planted, Apollos watered, but God gave the growth. So then neither the one who plants nor the one who waters is anything, but only God who gives the growth (1 Cor. 3:6-7).

What does it take for students to experience transformation from apathetic, passive, token Christians into vibrant, committed disciples? Is it possible to move from stagnation as a "group of youth" to vitality as a "student ministry"? Why do some churches seem to have all of the "really spiritual youth" who rise to levels of leadership, while others appear to attract only the "nominal church kids and their friends who like pizza," who may or may not show up on any given Sunday? For youth leaders to facilitate the spiritual transformation of youth, both individually and collectively, is not only possible, but it is our mandate as student ministers. How can this be accomplished? The solution is also the methodology—discipleship. God calls all Christians to be actively involved in this task of disciple-making.

Notice that the command with the Great Commission is not just to garner converts, but to make disciples, to teach the importance of obedience to Christ's teaching. Teaching suggests that learning is taking place. After all, if change does not take place in the lives of the learners, can we say we are really teaching, or that we are fulfilling the Great Commission to make disciples? It may seem to be an impossible task, to teach in such a way that brings about spiritual change in the lives of our students. We must remember, however, that we are not responsible for the change, and we do not approach the task of making disciples in our own power. It is the Holy Spirit who moves in the lives of believers to quicken the Word of God. It is the Holy Spirit who teaches through us when we seek His guidance and trust His power. Jesus promised He would always be with us. As youth leaders, we are called to be faithful to what God asks us to do.

The Meaning of Discipleship

It would be difficult to find a youth minister who did not identify discipleship as a key component of his or her ministry. Unfortunately, what passes for discipleship is often little more than a gathering of youth at the feet of a talking head, or "small groups" meeting in homes for food, fun, and a hastily-uttered devotion, followed by a time of share and prayer. Discipleship events sometimes rise to the level of excellent biblical content, but still fall short of disciple-making because the model of delivery or lack of application renders it ineffective in the lives of students. As student ministers, we must be good stewards of the opportunities we have to help youth grow as disciples of Jesus Christ. This means we should have a sense of what we seek to accomplish; an understanding of our mission.

Discipleship is not a structure or a plan or a lesson or an event. It is a commitment, a process, a way of life. Sunday evening at 6:00 p.m. is not discipleship; a weekend retreat is not discipleship; Tuesday evening small groups are not discipleship. These are all forms, or structures, which may *facilitate* discipleship, but they are no more discipleship than a church building is the church. Discipleship is the quality of *being* a disciple, in the same way that leadership is exercising the qualities of being a leader. Just as studying the qualities and processes of leadership doesn't make a person a leader, learning about the qualities of a disciple doesn't make a person a disciple. Discipleship programs or methods are the techniques we employ to work with God in growing disciples.

Basic Student Ministry

According to Gene Mims, "Discipleship is a lifelong journey of obedience to Christ that transforms a person's values and behavior and results in ministry in one's home, church, and the world." He adds that, "Discipling is the process of teaching the new citizen in the kingdom of God to love, trust, and obey the King and how to win and train others to do the same."[1] A disciple is a student, a learner; one who is committed to the Master and to learning about Him and from Him. A disciple embraces Christlike qualities and is a fully devoted follower of Christ in every area of life. It should be apparent from this description that discipleship cannot be mastered in a few months, or even a few years. It is a lifelong endeavor and it should be undertaken with a seriousness and an intensity rarely understood and practiced in the modern church or in the lives of most believers.[2]

As student ministers, our role is to implement a strategy that will move students from their current levels of commitment toward ever-deepening faith maturity and eventually into a role as a "multiplier" themselves. To do this effectively, we must:
- Crystallize our understanding of the characteristics of a true disciple
- Distinguish between levels of commitment, or stages of discipleship
- Develop a system for assessing the discipleship levels of our students
- Utilize strategies and methods for helping students realize growth as disciples
- Equip parents and adult leaders to assist in the disciple-making process
- Faithfully model the life of a growing disciple for our students
- Pray consistently for wisdom as we remain faithful to our role of equippers

Discipleship and Evangelism

Discipleship and evangelism are inseparable. The acceptance of the good news of salvation is traditionally considered the beginning of discipleship, the departure point for a lifelong journey with Christ. Many, however, accept a concept of pre-discipleship in which a person begins to learn about Christ and grow in understanding before making a personal commitment to follow Him in obedience. For them, evangelistic encounters are a form of discipleship. Regardless of where you mark the beginning point, evangelism is foundational to discipleship. From another vantage point, we can view evangelism as the fruit of a commitment to Christ. The obedience of disciples leads to evangelism.

Youth leaders should identify a discipleship method for reaching lost and unchurched youth. Big events for large groups of students can contribute to the making of disciples, when they are planned intentionally and supported with prayer. Committed Christian youth should be trained to build meaningful relationships with non-Christians and to share their faith stories. Not all recreational events are discipleship, but the potential for disciple-making is there.

From Crowd to Group to Committed to Multipliers

Your students will fall into one of at least four levels of commitment: the "Crowd," the "Group," the "Committed," and the "Multipliers." These commitment levels should not be confused with the spiritual maturity of a person, but considered a target category of youth you will want to address with specific discipleship methodologies. As you plan your discipleship approach, you will need to consider how to move

In youth ministry there is a tendency to try and do many things well. As noble as that may seem, I have discovered it is better to focus on fewer things and strive, with God's help, to do them exceptionally well. One of the areas where this is most obvious is in our youth discipleship ministry. We have made a conscious effort to put a major portion of our budget, training, and time to developing our discipleship ministry. In the discipleship process, students learn how to study God's Word, how to share their faith, discover and utilize their spiritual gifts, study and plan for involvement in missions, and also learn what it means to be involved in accountable relationships. All of this helps to strengthen every aspect of our total youth ministry program. Sunday School is our outreach arm, our midweek service builds unity, and our discipleship program is the foundation, which builds and feeds into all of the other programs.
—**Seth Buckley, minister to students, First Baptist Church, Spartanburg, South Carolina**

You shall love the Lord your God with all your heart, with all your soul, with all your strength, and with all your mind (Luke 10:27; See also Deut. 6:5).

your students from where they are to the next level of commitment, both as a group but more importantly as individuals.

Understand that when you assist students in their movement to deeper levels through the power of the Holy Spirit, it doesn't mean they won't occasionally fall back to a more basic level. These levels are not static and they really reflect increasing levels of love, trust, and obedience. It could be likened to individuals' responses to a body of water. Those who walk along the shore, daring occasionally to wade in are like the "Crowd." Others venture out into the water for a swim upon the surface ("Group"). Still others drop beneath the surface to snorkel for brief periods of time but are still tied to the surface ("Committed"). Finally there are those who spend most of their time beneath the surface as divers ("Multipliers"). It may be difficult to know the depth of your students. The best indication of their level of commitment is their love, trust, and obedience to Christ.

THE CROWD

The "Crowd" consists of all the students in the youth group plus their friends and any student to whom a local church has the potential to minister. Dr. Luke wrote of the feeding of the five thousand in chapter 9 of his gospel. Not that the number of "Crowd" teenagers represented in your youth group will be five thousand. In fact, the number in the New Testament was likely several times the five thousand that was reported, as only the men were counted (v. 14). But they represent a people group Jesus targeted at a beginning level of discipleship. Jesus and His disciples had returned to a place near a small town called Bethsaida (*beth-SAY ih duh*) on the north shore of the Sea of Galilee. As would be predictable with miracle workers, the crowds found Jesus, so He taught them. At the end of the day, Jesus instructed the disciples to feed the hungry people. More than likely these people were hungry for something spiritual to make a difference in their lives—even if they weren't sure how to define the emptiness they felt. They were hungry, both spiritually and physically, and Jesus healed some of them and fed all of them.

The Bible doesn't indicate that all of these people became devout disciples of Jesus, and we would not expect it. They represented several levels of commitment. All received a meal, some received healing, but it would be unrealistic by first or twenty-first century standards to believe that all continued to follow Christ. Most were content to gaze at the water while others dared to wade in. Some moved to more substantial depths of commitment.

- Crowd (5000)
- Group (70)
- Committed (12)
- Multiplier (3)

Just as Jesus challenged them on the hillside, the youth minister's job is to capture the imagination of these students. Help them see what their

Basic Student Ministry

lives might become if they were committed followers of Christ. Most of these students have no ability to feed themselves. Any spiritual nourishment they receive will likely be spoon-fed. The key for discipleship with these students is to introduce them to a relationship with Christ and assimilate them into the group at a beginning or foundational level of discipleship (help them move from the "Crowd" to the "Group" of followers who are taking the next steps of obedience).

THE GROUP

The "Group" is made up of those students who are normally involved in the ministry of the church (those considered a part of the youth group). In most cases, these students already have a relationship with Christ and with other believers and are beyond a beginning level of discipleship, but they are still at a basic level. Later, in Luke 10, this is likely the group in whom Jesus invested as the end of His earthly ministry drew near. He told this visitation team that the harvest is abundant but the workers are few (10:2). He warned them of the possibility of being unwelcomed and presenting a message that would be met with hostility. Some of them—possibly all of them—understood the urgency of their mission. They were part of the larger group of disciples, competent to prepare the towns for the upcoming visits Jesus would make. There is no indication that these 35 teams of 2 were otherwise remarkable. They had seen Jesus' power and were willing to trust Him.

"Group" students can usually eat solid spiritual food if someone gives it to them—as was the case with Jesus and His 70 followers. The challenge for this group is to take ownership of their faith, to make it theirs. They have already begun to take the next important steps of maturing as disciples by becoming part of ministry teams. Through their obedience to Jesus' challenge, they began to mature in their likeness to Christ. They have, in a sense, pushed out from the shore and are actively swimming in the pool of ministry.

THE COMMITTED

The "Committed" is actually the first group mentioned in Luke 9 and is identified as "the Twelve." They were a separate group from the larger body of disciples, named in Luke 6 and Mark 3. Jesus delegated authority to them for certain tasks. The word *apostle* is used of those twelve disciples whom Jesus sent out, two by two, during His ministry in Galilee to expand His own ministry of preaching and healing. (See also Mark 3:14; 6:30.) But the Twelve were included in most of the intimate conversations and ministry experiences with Jesus. According to church tradition, they all, save one, became leaders of churches.

These students (likely more or less than 12) are growing and ready for advanced discipleship. Though they still have much to learn, as was the case with the Twelve, they can feed themselves and are involved in multiplying ministry—reproducing other disciples and bearing fruit. These students can go deeper, at least for short periods of time. They are equipped with snorkeling equipment that sustains them for excursions beneath the waves, but aren't really ready to remain there for extended periods of time. The questions they ask and the way they live may suggest a need for the basics, but these students are generally underchallenged and in need of advanced discipleship. Our job is to raise the bar.

THE MULTIPLIERS

The "Multipliers" are made up of teenagers who are ready to feed others and move beyond simply participating in ministry teams to actually leading these teams. It represents a very

> "For everyone who calls on the name of the Lord will be saved." But how can they call on Him in whom they have not believed? And how can they believe without hearing about Him? And how can they hear without a preacher? And how can they preach unless they are sent? (Rom. 10:13-15a).

small proportion of your youth ministry. In Luke 9, Scripture says Jesus took Peter, James, and John to a mountain (either Mount Hermon or Mount Tabor) for an incredibly special retreat. We don't know why He singled these three out. Maybe they were more spiritually tuned in than the other nine. The words they heard Jesus say in the eight days between the feeding of the five thousand and the transfiguration were tough words, and their response was certainly favorable. Maybe it was because they were some of the first among the ones called (Luke 1:16). They were also present at some miracles the others missed (Luke 8:51). One could take this one step further by examining the specific words Jesus had for one disciple, Simon Peter (Luke 9:18-27). Jesus never understood the needs of His followers to be identical and neither should we. The youth minister's job with these students is to help them discover their areas of giftedness and provide opportunities to serve and to lead in service. They, too, should not only be challenged at an advanced discipleship level but also engaged in leadership development.

Assessing the Needs of Your Students

Though not exhaustive, the following list can help you assess the spiritual maturity of your youth. It is a basic overview of the qualities and characteristics of a growing disciple, based on the teachings of Scripture and what a multiplying believer should know, be, and do.

- *Salvation.*—Do your students understand the nature of sin and the need for salvation? Have they made a public faith commitment to Christ? Do their actions reflect their commitment?
- *Bible.*—Do your students have a growing knowledge of biblical teachings? Do they value the Bible as the literal Word of God? Are they involved in Scripture memory and personal Bible study? Are they faithful in attendance in Sunday School and other opportunities for corporate Bible study? Do they apply biblical teachings to their lives?
- *Prayer.*—Do your students exhibit a knowledge of biblical teachings about prayer? Do they speak about the power of prayer in their lives? Are they willing to pray publicly? Do they have a consistent daily time alone with God?
- *Church.*—Do your students understand the importance of the body of Christ? Are they committed to regular attendance and participation in the body? Do they actively participate in the life of the church? Do they have an understanding and appreciation for the historical teachings and practices of the church?
- *Spiritual Gifts.*—Do your students understand giftedness? Are they interested in discovering their unique gifts? Do they seek ways in which they can use their gifts in personal ministry? Do they use their gifts to build up the body?
- *Witness.*—Do your students know how to share their faith? Are they committed to sharing their personal faith stories with the lost? Do they consistently seek opportunities to reach lost friends? Are they burdened for those who are lost?
- *Stewardship.*—Do your students understand biblical teachings about stewardship? Are they committed to living responsibly as faithful stewards of their time, talents, and material resources? Do their actions match their commitments?

- *Relationships.*—Do your students attempt to relate to others as representatives of Christ? Do they seek to love others as Christ loves them? Do they treat others with love and respect? Do they show respect for authority? Are they committed to the value of all persons?
- *Creation.*—Do your students understand the significance of creation? Do they value life unconditionally? Do they actively care for God's creation?
- *Lifestyle.*—Do your students know what it means to live as Christians in a sinful world? Are they committed to living according to biblical standards of morality? Are their lifestyle decisions consistent with biblical teachings?
- *Service*—Do your students understand the biblical teachings about ministry? Do they practice servant leadership? Do they use their gifts to serve others? Are they committed to justice, mercy, love, and humility? Do they volunteer to participate in ministry and mission endeavors? Do they recognize ministry needs in the world?

Disciples are living, growing persons. They progress through stages of spiritual maturity, just as they grow and develop physically, emotionally, and mentally. While there are no set times or age limits for attaining specific levels of faith maturity, it is important to realize that growth in discipleship needs to be nurtured throughout life. It is possible for Christians to become stagnant in their faith, or stunted in their growth. For this reason, youth leaders have a serious responsibility to discover the spiritual maturity level of each of their students and to provide consistent nourishment. Some students will be at the initial faith commitment stage (beginning) and require spiritual "milk" as members of the "Crowd." Others will be ready to "feed themselves" but will need to be taught how to do this (basic) as members of the "Group." There will be students who have a solid commitment to take responsibility for their own growth as followers of Christ, but will still need accountability and guidance to ensure that they are "eating healthy food" (advanced) as members of the "Committed." Some students will be solidly committed to Christ and growing as healthy disciples. They need deeper challenges and opportunities to develop their capacity to feed and nurture others who are still spiritual babies.

The process of formal and informal evaluation is invaluable in helping youth leaders assess the relative spiritual growth of their youth. "In order for believers to minister effectively, they must be transformed in Christ (be), they must know the truth (know), and they must have the skills and/or spiritual gifts to minister effectively (do)."[3] Once you determine what a disciple should know, be, and do, and then assess how your students measure up to this standard, you can implement a plan to help them become growing disciples by addressing these issues with specific methods of discipleship.

Discipleship and Church Practice

The function of discipleship, like the other functions of the church, encompasses all the strategies of church practice. What follows is a description of how discipleship can be fleshed out through the church practice.

CLOSED GROUP STRATEGY

The bulk of discipleship that happens in a local church and its youth ministry is within the confines of closed groups. "A closed-group strategy exists to build kingdom leaders and to equip believers to serve by engaging people in discipleship that moves them toward spiritual transformation through short-term, self-contained, training units in an atmos-

The Value of Small Group Discipleship in Youth Ministry

A high school coach wrote in my yearbook something I will never forget. He said, "Mike, there are three things in life: good, better, and best. Never settle for less than the best." I am of the opinion the best method to achieve the end goal of "presenting students mature in Christ" is through small groups. Large group discipleship is good.

The Christian life is about becoming more like Jesus. Life change is the goal not the acquiring of information. High accountability within small groups is more likely to achieve life change. Romans 8:29 reads, "For those He foreknew He also predestined to be conformed to the image of His Son." The small group of four or less students is better equipped to facilitate the process of accountability needed to help us grow to be more like Christ.

Most youth ministries I have seen or heard about define a small group as 6-12 students. I have found 4 or less to be a much more effective size. Desiring greater life change led me to the smaller group in my early years of youth ministry. The investment of Jesus through your life into the lives of students happens more effectively when the leader has fewer students.

Accountability should be checked concerning attitude and actions at home, school,

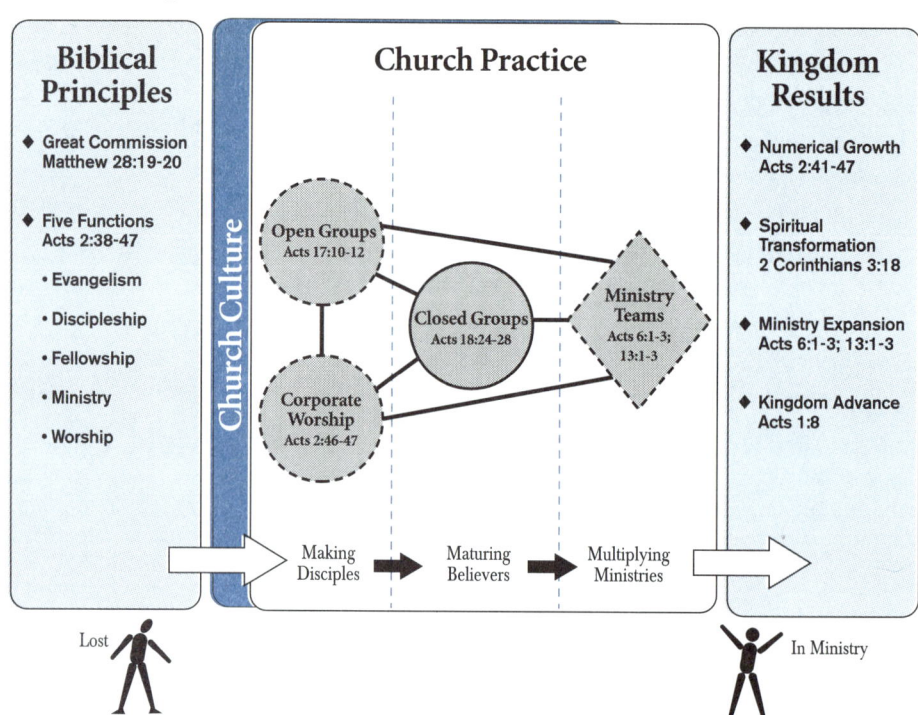

phere of accountability to God and to each other."⁴ A successful strategy for closed groups is person-centered, lay-led, and Bible-based that equips teenagers for kingdom ministry. Mostly these groups are designed to equip leaders for ministry. It is because of this emphasis that the discipleship, training, and equipping for ministry teams will be done in a closed group setting. The focus of these closed groups is on believers who need maturity for ministry rather than to reach unbelievers and believers alike in order to teach, evangelize, and assimilate as is the case for open groups.⁵

Covenant Groups

Covenant groups are a part of a closed group strategy and require students to commit to attendance. They also demand they commit to personal study outside of the regular meeting time. Such groups are important to help students grow beyond a spiritual plateau. An hour a week of learning how to be a disciple will not result in committed student disciples, mature in their faith. Covenant groups help students put their intentions into actions. Due to the more intense nature of the studies, covenant groups very often last longer than four weeks. These groups may meet at any time or place during the week that best meets the time demands of the students, leaders, families, and church schedule. Students are informed of the responsibilities and requirements of participation in the study and agree to fulfill them. Such groups are designed for youth who are committed to spiritual growth. This is an excellent way to develop these committed students as leaders.

Basic Student Ministry

For this kind of high impact, covenant discipleship, many youth ministers are buying into the concept of a Discipleship Spider. A team of youth ministers with effective discipleship skills suggested eight elements that might make up the core or body of the Discipleship Spider: obedience to Christ; accountable relationships, priorities, Scripture, prayer, personal ministry, spiritual warfare, and Christlike character. They have suggested that youth ministers consider teaching a discipleship course on one of these elements, or spider legs, each school semester so students can finish the spider in four years.

Open Group and Corporate Worship Strategies

Though the bulk of discipleship in a church and youth ministry will happen through a closed group strategy, foundational discipleship should happen in open group and corporate worship strategies. Since open groups and corporate worship strategies target believers and unbelievers there must be an element of foundational discipleship in order to address the needs of believers (who never become too mature for foundational discipleship on a continual basis). On the other hand, since unbelievers are involved in open groups and worship, the discipleship must remain at a beginning or foundational level.

Sunday School classes, cell groups, short-term small group Bible studies such as Youth Vacation Bible School or youth camp, as well as new member classes are all usually focused on beginning discipleship. Thus, these would be considered to be a part of an open group strategy if they target saved and lost kids at the foundational level of discipleship. On the other hand, youth Wednesday night worship services, concerts, youth rallies, and youth evangelism conferences are excellent entry points for lost students, but also contain a foundational discipleship emphasis as part of the corporate worship strategy.

Ministry Team Strategy

Discipleship can happen through a ministry team strategy as well. It extends beyond the equipping for the particular ministry taking place. Doing ministry is an essential application of discipleship. It is the back end of spiritual transformation that is love, trust, and obedience—the "doing" of discipleship.

The adults in your church are at various stages of spiritual maturity, just as your students. This is to be expected, considering that some persons come to faith later in life. The tragedy is that many adults have made an initial faith commitment as children or youth, but have not grown as disciples. One strong factor in this spiritual stagnation may be that they were not involved in a youth ministry that provided them with a sound foundation of discipleship. Youth need opportunities to discover their spiritual gifts and utilize them in service before reaching adulthood. Ministry teams are an excellent way to assist students in their growth as disciples.

Students with similar or complementary gifts may be enlisted to serve together to accomplish a specific ministry purpose. These teams may include such responsibilities as discovering the needs of your students, ministry, church, and community and committing themselves to pray faithfully for these needs. This prayer team might also be responsible for bringing the prayer needs to the attention of the group and planning and implementing prayer strategies for the entire ministry. Students with gifts in administration and planning may take the lead in helping to develop the calendar or ministry details. Drama and music teams may assist in worship planning and leading. They may discover ways to utilize their gifts in ministry and outreach. Students with strong academic skills may develop a tutoring ministry for children or other youth.

and church. Everywhere the student touches lives a potential accounting should be asked for. It is extremely hard to hold a group of eight to this level of accountability.
—Michael Lundrum teaches youth ministry at North Greenville College in Greenville, South Carolina

There are no limits to the types or number of ministry teams that may exist within a specific youth ministry. Some youth ministers, however, may choose to limit the number of ministry teams an individual student may participate in within a given time frame. Students who overextend themselves or leave no time to interact with family may experience frustration if they are not able to minister effectively due to time demands. Over-commitment can also lead to unnecessary stress or feelings of inadequacy or failure.

Not all students are ready for participation on some ministry teams. They should not be formed on the basis of popularity, nor should the impression be given that team members are "special" or "spiritual giants." Christian leadership is about servanthood, and ministry teams are opportunities for students to serve. They help in the transformation of students from passive members of a youth ministry to active Christians utilizing their gifts in service. As such, they are an integral component of an effective discipleship strategy.

Small youth ministries may have difficulty forming youth ministry teams until they begin experiencing numerical and/or spiritual growth. This should not keep individual youth from serving in specific areas of ministry leadership or serving on adult ministry teams in other areas of the church. One youth may have a heart for ministry, and may be used by God to motivate the other students to action. As the youth minister, it is urgent that you identify ways some of your students can plug into the ministry action of your local church. Your responsibility as a youth leader is to assist in the spiritual growth of each youth in your care. Sometimes this requires extra creativity and flexibility in your strategy.

Discipleship Methods

Following is a list of possible methods for discipling the students in your church within the context of the four church practice strategies. Remember that discipleship is not a structure or a plan, a lesson or an event. It is a way of life. Methods are only means by which we can equip students for the way of life, they aren't discipleship. Many of the following methods can be implemented through any of the four church practice strategies, depending on the people group you are targeting and the desired outcome of the method. Consider which methodology works best with the target group ("Crowd," "Group," "Committed," or "Multiplier") you are trying to disciple. This is certainly not an exhaustive list of discipleship methodologies but contains some important things to remember as you use methods for practicing strategy.

BIBLE STUDY

To grow in Christlikeness, students need an understanding of who Christ is. The Bible is the primary source for this knowledge. It is not enough for students to read and study the Gospels, for to fully understand Christ's identity, nature, purpose, work, and teachings, it is necessary to study the entire Word of God. Ongoing comprehensive Bible study is a foundational component of discipleship and should be a cornerstone of any youth ministry. Youth leaders need to help students develop a commitment and love for inductive Bible study, where the focus is on the passage and its meaning in context. Seek to read and understand the truth of the Bible, then ask God to reveal its meaning for you and your students. Careful evaluation and selection of Bible study resources is an important step in the process of disciple-making. (See Appendix 2 for a sample checklist.)

Bible study can be accomplished in large groups, but the dynamics of a small group are most effective in helping students to appropriate meaning. (See the sidebar on p. 38.) Closed, or covenant group Bible studies, may occasionally be recommended for "Committed" or "Multiplier" students, if some form of accountability is a desired outcome. Open groups target "Crowd" students as well as the other teen people groups in ongoing small group settings. Bible study in these settings should be aimed at foundational evangelism and foundational discipleship.

Ongoing Topical Groups

There are specific truths and skills all Christians need to "master" if they are to mature in their faith. For example, students need to develop personal spiritual disciplines such as prayer and Bible study. They need to understand how to make wise decisions as stewards of God's resources. There are also biblical attitudes and values that need to be nurtured, such as love, humility, and patience. Sometimes specific situations arise that youth ministers need to address from a biblical vantage point. Such situations may include violent death or suicide, rape or other forms of violence, natural disasters, or family troubles. Ongoing/short-term groups can meet any of these needs.

There may be a specific time of the week, such as Sunday evening, when you may incorporate ongoing groups into your youth ministry strategy. This may be one that will systematically cover a wide variety of topics and issues that will be relevant to all youth. Some youth ministers identify a few key study topics that are needed by all youth and schedule these topical groups to run simultaneously, with youth selecting the course that most appeals to them at the time. Most short-term topical studies such as these will run approximately four to six weeks, then they could be repeated so that all youth are given the opportunity for involvement in each study. The advantage of such an approach is that the groups can remain small and intimate, and may be tailored to fit a specific age group or church practice strategy with a beginning, basic, or advanced level approach. Leaders could be enlisted to lead one specific study repeatedly, allowing them to focus their preparation time. Discipleship studies offered in this manner are most effective when they allow youth to enter at any time during the multiple-week study.

Individual Study

There are some students who are ready for deeper levels of discipleship development than their peers. Sometimes complicated schedules prohibit youth from participating in traditional ongoing groups. In such cases, you may elect to provide individual youth with a discipleship resource they can study on their own, a self-directed study. To maximize spiritual growth and provide accountability, it is advisable to match individual students with an adult mentor who will meet with them or make contact with them weekly.

Accountability partners and opportunities for mentoring are increasingly recognized as important, but often overlooked, components of the disciple-making process. There are many adults who cannot commit to regular group leadership on a weekly basis, but who would be willing to invest their lives in the life of a teenager. Sometimes "Multiplier" students can serve in this role for younger or newer Christian students in your group. This type of relationship is especially significant for youth who do not have stable or consistent Christian role models in their homes. You may select discipleship resources to guide the accountability or mentoring process, or simply provide guidelines for their interaction that will propel your students toward spiritual growth.

EVENTS AND TRIPS

Events and trips can be significant methods for the spiritual growth of "Crowd" students if they are planned carefully with a clearly defined goal. When planning events or short-term projects, ask yourself such questions as these:

- Is the context "Christian"—will the project detract from the intended purpose?
- Does the experience allow for good stewardship of God's resources of time, money, talents, and possessions?
- Will the experience connect them or alienate them from the collective body of Christ?
- Are the leaders worthy mentors and spiritual examples?
- Are the youth spiritually prepared, in order to advance God's purposes and not to hinder them?
- Is time allowed in the schedule for reflection and integration of the experience with scriptural principles?
- Is there a sound rationale for the experience, or does it just have popular appeal?
- Is this event or trip allowing youth to join God in His work?
- Will the event cause divisions within the body or promote harmony?
- Will this provide a context for moving youth forward in their faith maturity or simply fill their calendars?
- Will some youth be left out due to their social status, family, or economic conditions?
- Will youth be given opportunities to use their spiritual gifts?

DISCIPLENOW

A discipleship event for the "Crowd" (all youth who have a connection with your ministry), which has proven to be extremely effective, is a focused retreat known as a DiscipleNow. The DiscipleNow retreat is designed for small groups of students to meet in homes with a leader for an entire weekend. Each small group typically studies the same focused content, based on a specified theme. Staying together in a home for a concentrated period of time allows students to develop relationships and focus on one particular need of discipleship, without the distractions of the outside world. It is also an excellent way to tie in the entire youth ministry to the church, since adults are enlisted to provide meals for the student groups and to provide transportation for any scheduled recreation or service projects you might incorporate into the schedule. During the weekend, the small group leaders will also meet individually with each student for a time of spiritual assessment, accountability, and informal mentoring. DiscipleNows that are aimed at the

And He personally gave some to be apostles, some prophets, some evangelists, some pastors and teachers, for the training of the saints in the work of ministry, to build up the body of Christ, until we all reach unity in the faith and in the knowledge of God's Son, [growing] into a mature man with a stature measured by Christ's fullness. Then we will no longer be little children, tossed by the waves and blown around by every wind of teaching, by human cunning with cleverness in the techniques of deceit. (Eph. 4:11-14).

"Committed" or "Multipliers" are a part of a closed group strategy. The idea is to offer specialized and advanced level training for these students that would be inappropriate for the lost or beginning level disciples. The culmination event of a DiscipleNow is a celebratory worship service, involving the entire church congregation. Youth are given leadership responsibilities for the service and are encouraged to publicly share all spiritual decisions and faith commitments made during the course of the weekend.

CAMPS AND RETREATS

Camps and retreats can be planned to meet various needs of your youth ministry, including targeted foundational discipleship needs for your "Crowd" students. You may want to focus on prayer or spiritual gifts, for example, and select a discipleship resource to utilize as a foundation for your Bible study times. Games, recreation, and worship times can then be planned to emphasize your study, or to provide opportunities for youth to reflect upon or put into practice what they have been learning. Again, if your aim is to pull some of your youth leadership or committed students away for some time of intense, advanced discipleship training, then the method would fit into a closed group strategy.

SERVICE AND MISSIONS

Service projects and mission trips are also effective methods for helping your students grow as disciples. The benefits of being involved in volunteer ministries have been identified as deepening religious faith, integrating faith and social ministry, increasing leadership abilities and self-confidence, contributing to church and missions commitment, helping participants understand the role of the church in society, building a sense of community with other Christians, developing cultural sensitivity and appreciation, enhancing self-worth and self-concept, developing values, and increasing one's dependence on God. These are all desired qualities of a disciple. Ministry projects are often preferable to youth camps for the purpose of discipleship, because it gives students the opportunity to serve, instead of being the recipients of service.

The positive discipleship impact of ministry involvement is not limited to individual youth and those whom they serve. There are benefits to sponsoring youth groups and churches, as well. Congregations frequently report increased youth group cohesion and commitment to service as a result of involvement. Key components in building this sense of group include a shared task and purpose and the need for interdependence to accomplish goals. Other group benefits are the application of biblical learning to real life, the empowerment of youth for leadership, and the shift in role expectations of adult leaders from presenters of information to facilitators of faith learning. Churches that provide opportunities for youth to become involved in ministry are giving them a chance to explore and use their spiritual gifts and talents. Idealism is a developmental characteristic of youth, and churches and youth ministries that provide an outlet for youth to act on this idealism attract large numbers of teenagers. Numerical growth is one measure of an effective discipleship strategy.

The greatest benefits from mission projects are derived when youth are given the opportunity to reflect on their experiences. Many of the claims made about the benefits of service are not true if youth are not given the opportunity to reflect critically on the process. Reflection can actually multiply the commitment to missions and ministry. Opportunities to reflect publicly on their experiences (such as in a worship service) also promote the leadership skills of young disciples.

When we are truly disciples, Jesus will be allowed to touch others through us. This practice of the presence of God in our lives should lead to a life of serving others (Matt. 22:37-39). I am not sure who to credit for this saying, but it is so true: "We are Christians, not by what we do, but by whom we obey." Discipleship is surrender to an awesome God every moment of every day! Teenagers, filled with all the emotions and pressures of the day, need a personal example of a true disciple, to form the foundation for any formal learning experience. Yes, it involves sacrifice, and OH YEAH, JOY!
—Charlie Dodd, youth minister, First Baptist Church; Midland, Texas

And Jesus called them over and said to them, "You know that those who are regarded as rulers of the Gentiles dominate them, and their men of high position exercise power over them. But it must not be so among you. On the contrary, whoever wants to become great among you must be your servant, and whoever wants to be first among you must be a slave to all. For even the Son of Man did not come to be served, but to serve, and to give His life–a ransom for many" (Mark 10:42-45).

Special service and mission events and trips are excellent means of helping your students grow in discipleship, but there are specific events that should only be open to your "Committed" youth, or "Multiplier" students. Some mission trips fall into this category, because of the level of commitment and leadership required of the participants. Local ministry or service projects can help the "Group" or the "Crowd" develop a heart and passion to love and serve in the name of Jesus. For longer or more intense specific mission efforts, it may be imperative that students have a level of spiritual maturity commiserate with the task, if the kingdom of God is to be advanced and not hindered.

LEADERSHIP DEVELOPMENT

Covenant groups, individual mentoring, and ministry teams are key ways to assist in the development of students into leaders. Some youth leaders identify specific youth as student leaders and give them responsibilities and greater individual attention. A word of caution: *Students tend to equate leadership with status and authority. Christian leadership is about humility and service. Take care that you don't contribute to the spiritual arrogance of youth, or cause divisions or jealousy within your ministry.* Jesus dealt with this issue among the Twelve, after the mother of James and John requested that they be given seats of honor in His kingdom. To quell the division of the group, Jesus challenged them to consider servanthood (Mark 10:35-45).

If you choose to identify student leaders for a specific purpose, make sure that they are selected on the basis of well-defined spiritual and lifestyle criteria. Clearly define their tasks and your expectations, and hold them accountable in all areas. If there is not a critical need for a student leader group, then it is best to develop the leadership potential of "Multiplier" students through ministry teams and covenant groups. Not everyone can rise to the level of leadership, but all students can develop leadership skills in the kingdom. It would be tragic to identify some students as leaders and not recognize the potential in others.

What specific attitudes, behaviors, and skills do you want to develop in student leaders? In addition to basic discipleship characteristics, leadership requires training in specific areas, such as:

- Biblical understanding of servant leadership
- Leading through giftedness
- Exemplifying the fruit of the Spirit as a leader
- How to motivate and lead others
- Mentoring and accountability skills
- Basic skills in listening and communicating
- Peer counseling techniques
- Conflict resolution
- How to prepare and lead Bible studies
- Delegation skills
- Understanding of group dynamics
- Decision-making skills
- Vocational ministry discernment
- Character development

These topics can be addressed through closed, small group settings that would include: conferences, video sessions, short-term sessions, or retreats. The most effective way to develop these skills in your students is by modeling first, then allowing them to practice or implement the behaviors/skills. Debrief their experiences, encouraging, affirming, and providing constructive criticism. As they continue to learn while they lead, their skills will become refined and more effective. Students who exhibit high levels of competence may then begin to teach and mentor their peers in these same skills.

Parental Involvement

The most important and influential relationships in the lives of your students remain the relationships they have with their parents. The primary spiritual leaders in the lives of children should be their parents. God intended this from the beginning and has given parents specific instructions to train and nurture their children in the faith. Unfortunately, the reality of our society is such that parents rarely fulfill this role. As youth leaders, we are called to assist parents in this task, not to attempt to replace them. How can you help make disciples of students and also help parents assume this responsibility?

A very basic consideration of youth leaders should be to teach with an awareness of the biblical role of the family. This means students must be taught to communicate with, respect, and honor their parents. Sometimes they need help in learning how to relate to parents who do not have a relationship with Christ or who do not live out their faith. Youth leaders can help create opportunities for parents and youth to grow together in their commitment to Christ. Discipleship training can cross generational boundaries allowing students to study with their parents. This may be accomplished through structured small groups, by providing discipleship resources to be used in the home, or planning a discipleship retreat or ministry projects for youth and parents together.

Seth Buckley of First Baptist Church Spartanburg, South Carolina, had traditionally included a youth discipleship weekend in his yearly plan. While many parents attended as sponsors and workers, the training and worship were designed to help the students grow as disciples. Recently, Seth has begun to focus the retreat on discipleship training for both youth and parents. Recreation, meals, and worship times were together, but separate training classes were designed for youth and their parents. The first such retreat included more than 400 youth and 120 parents. Parents were then encouraged to participate in ongoing discipleship small groups that were structured to meet their diverse needs. This was not planned in isolation, but the pastor and other age-group ministers were also in attendance and supported the efforts of the student ministry to help in the disciple-making process of parents of youth.

Developing and Implementing Your Plan

When you consider the discipleship needs of your students, you may feel overwhelmed. Keep in mind that not everything can be done at once, and that the results are not your responsibility. Your task is to remain faithful to what God requires of you, and then to get out of the way and allow Him to work. It takes time to assess the spiritual development of students. It takes time to develop an approach for helping students to maximize their spiritual growth. It takes wisdom to assess and strategize effectively, which can only come through conversations with the Father. Nurture your own spiritual growth, seek out an accountability for yourself, don't neglect spiritual disciplines in your life, model the attitudes and behaviors you desire, and listen to the voice of the Holy Spirit for guidance.

After you have clearly defined your discipleship goals and assessed your students' levels of spiritual growth, you must then begin to determine how you will format your discipleship approach. What is the best structure to meet the needs? What resources will best address the needs? How will you identify leaders? How will you involve parents? How will you plan for continual growth instead of shotgun solutions? Charlie Dodd of First Baptist Midland, Texas, has one of the most comprehensive plans for youth discipleship I have encountered. Simply put, he and his volunteers have carefully developed a long-range strategy of disciple-making that takes into consideration every facet of biblical discipleship they have identified. They then pair each facet with each year a student will be involved in the youth ministry. This plan, or taxonomy, provides for a comprehensive program of discipleship training for all youth, from the "Crowd" to "Multipliers." Each ministry is unique, but the requirements of a disciple are not. All are called to the same biblical standard of growth and faithfulness. Youth leaders are responsible for creating their own strategy, one which will contribute to the spiritual growth of the students.

Characteristics of a True Disciple

How do you evaluate the spiritual maturity of your students? When you think about your youth, whom would you identify as a committed disciple? The one who is faithful in attendance, always there? The student who engages in discussion, who has the right answers? The youth who participated in Bible Drill and can still recite hundreds of verses and recall their references? Or is it the student who invites the most friends to outreach events? The one who has an even temperament and gets along with everyone? Do you think about the youth who speaks passionately about Jesus as best friend? Is it the student who leads others in musical praise and worship with passionate sincerity? What about that youth who always volunteers to pray? The one who volunteers for ministry opportunities sponsored by your church?

A disciple is not identified only by what he or she knows, or values, or does. It is the combination of knowledge, attitude, and behaviors that mark a true disciple. Discipleship involves total life commitment, and life cannot be neatly compartmentalized. Our thoughts influence our beliefs, attitudes, values, and behaviors, and vice versa. Both the Old and New Testaments teach us the importance of loving God with our total beings.

There are vital truths, commitments, and behaviors, which should be evident in the life of a growing disciple. They are the fruit of a life of faith. Students who remain in Christ, attached to the true Vine, will grow and bear such fruit. The test of an effective program of discipleship is found in the lives of the students. Are they growing and bearing fruit? Leaders who are concerned about accomplishing the Great Commission, making authentic disciples, must critically evaluate the outcomes of their strategies, as evidenced by the lives of their students.

[1] Gene Mims, *Kingdom Principles for Church Growth*, Nashville: LifeWay Press, 2001, 39.
[2] Ibid, 40.
[3] Gene Mims, *The Kingdom-Focused Church*, Nashville: Broadman & Holman, 2003, 143.
[4] Mims, 2001, 110.
[5] Mims, 2003, 142-143.

"I am the vine; you are the branches. The one who remains in Me and I in him produces much fruit, because you can do nothing without Me. If anyone does not remain in Me, he is thrown aside like a branch and he withers. They gather them, throw them into the fire, and they are burned. If you remain in Me and My words remain in you, ask whatever you want and it will be done for you. My Father is glorified by this: that you produce much fruit and prove to be My disciples" (John 15:5-8).

chapter 3

FELLOWSHIP

Rick Morton

> *Fellowship is more than just a feeling of goodwill in a congregation. It is a result of the intimate spiritual relationship Christians share with God and other believers through their relationship with Jesus Christ. Fellowship doesn't evolve naturally in a community of believers, but comes only by the power of God working through and among them.*
> —Gene Mims, Vice President, LifeWay Church Resources

"WHEN I FIRST STARTED GOING to church here, I really liked the way people treated each other. It was . . . different . . . good. Not like other places. I really found some people who cared about me just for me. They really helped me see Jesus."

—Josh, 16
Louisville, Kentucky

The place of fellowship in student ministry almost goes without saying. In fact, let's be honest. Many of us have spent the balance of our student ministry years trying to shed the image of a "program director" or a "fellowship leader." I remember having the feeling as a young youth minister that many people thought fellowship was all I did or could be trusted to do. As a new youth minister, I bristled at that characterization. After all, I was called by God to do "serious ministry," and I had studied long and hard to know God's Word and to know teenagers. Teenagers are living in a very real and scary world, right? Many of them are living and dying apart from Christ, right? The task of ministry to today's youth is urgent. So, do we really have time for fun and games?

This is a really tough question. Difficult questions require thoughtful answers. To uncover the proper role of fellowship in ministry to students, I think we must consider a number of historical, biblical, and practical issues relating to fellowship.

> **And they devoted themselves to the apostles' teaching, to fellowship, to the breaking of bread, and to prayers . . . And every day they devoted themselves to meeting together in the temple complex, and broke bread from house to house. They ate their food with gladness and simplicity of heart, praising God and having favor with all the people (Acts 2:42,46-47).**

> *If anyone chooses to believe evangelism, discipleship, ministry, and worship are the essential functions of the church, that person must believe that fellowship is the incubator for their success.*
> —Gene Mims, Vice President, LifeWay Church Resources

Fellowship in Youth Ministry History

From the very beginning of the history of church work with youth, fellowship, relationship building, and community have been centerpieces of church practice. With only a brief overview of the history of youth ministry, we can definitely identify some key fellowship trends that have affected the student ministry climate today. For instance, we can look back to the "youth rally strategies" that reigned supreme from the 1930s through the 1960s. These large-scale rallies were used by denominational and parachurch ministries to create a sense of excitement and to bring students together for ministry.[1] Continuing from the 1960s, local churches adopted this "event" use of fellowship and carried it forward on a smaller scale well into the 1990s. The formula for local churches using this style of ministry was pretty simple. First, churches would plan a ministry event (or a calendar full of ministry events) with popular appeal to both churched and unchurched teenagers. Second, they would promote the event with every available method through every conceivable outlet to teenagers. The third step had two real operating principles: (1) use the event to build relationships with unchurched students with the hope of creating opportunities to bring them to Christ and include them in the ministry of the church; and (2) use the event to excite students within the church, build relationships with them, encourage them in their walk with Christ, and give them a safe place to "hang out" and have fun. This formula may be a bit of an oversimplification, but it illustrates the place of fellowship in youth ministry for many years. By and large, fellowships were events organized to provide a "front door" to the church for students who were outside the church and at the same time to provide good, clean fun and a positive connection point for kids who were already a part of the ministry of the church.

While it cannot be denied that fellowship-based activity has been a part of student ministry from the beginning, the question of the appropriate type and degree of fellowship activities has risen greatly in the past decade or two. With a push from Saddleback Community Church and Doug Fields, youth ministers have all been challenged to consider both the biblical rationale for their ministry efforts and the resulting productivity of those efforts in meeting goals.[2] From this understanding of fellowship, I think we can come down to three essential questions with which we must deal. First, *What is God's eternal purpose for fellowship and how does that purpose relate to local church student ministry?* Second, *What are the appropriate tools and methods at our disposal for fostering biblical fellowship among the students we serve?* And finally, *How can these methods of fostering fellowship be used within the church strategies most churches already have in place to accomplish ministry?*

What Does the Bible Have to Say About Fellowship?

Getting a handle on the biblical understanding of fellowship can be a difficult and perplexing problem in the modern church and student ministry culture. Many questions arise such as: *How can student ministries be expected to prioritize "fun and games" when the issues facing today's young people are so great and time and resources are so limited? Do recreational activities for students serve any real purpose or have any lasting benefit?"* What is the *proper place of fellowship with the other biblical functions for ministry? Should biblical fellowship extend beyond recreation or social activities in student ministry?* With so many weighty questions, even the most seasoned student ministry leader can be left wondering about the proper function and application of fellowship as a part of a balanced student ministry. To complicate matters, many have confused the biblical purpose of Christian fellowship with an event or a meeting that is often called "a fellowship."

To understand the concept of fellowship properly and to determine its role within student ministry programming, fellowship must be defined. In the New Testament, the basic words translated as *fellowship* come from the Greek root *koin-*, which means *to share in something with someone*. Perhaps the general concept can best be understood from Jesus' words about the church in John 10:14-16. This fellowship or sharing among Christians described here is rooted in the individual believer's relationship to Jesus as Shepherd. From this understanding, it can be said that Christian fellowship is the process of sharing together in community with others who are also Christians. Inherently, the purpose of fellowship within the body of Christ (and by extension the youth group) is for individual members to grow closer in unity with Christ and His church.

Anyone who has ever worked with teenagers for more than five minutes knows the difficulty fostering unity among teenagers. Because of their growing independence and their insecurity with a developing self, many youth seem to find comfort (if not delight) in creating and cultivating factions or divisions for identification. So, you may be left to wonder: *I understand that fellowship is meant to draw the body of Christ (specifically my local student ministry) together and in unity with Christ, but how can that be achieved practically with students who at times seem determined to push everyone away?* To gain greater insight for answering that question, let's begin by looking at some biblical passages. These passages identify a number of intentional purposes for fellowship that can then be interpreted in light of the unique issues of adolescence and student ministry.

> "I am the good shepherd. I know My own sheep, and they know Me, as the Father knows Me, and I know the Father. I lay down my life for the sheep. But I have other sheep that are not of this fold; I must bring them also, and they will listen to my voice. Then there will be one flock, one shepherd" (John 10:14-16).

Jesus' Example for Fellowship

There is no better example of ministry than the accounts of Jesus' earthly ministry. By looking to Jesus' example with His followers, we can understand at least four principles for building fellowship in student ministry.

Create a place where students are known. People (especially teens) need an environment where they are known for who they really are and allowed to be themselves. Matthew 9:9-13, tells the account of Jesus' call of Matthew. Jesus called Matthew right out of a dubious profession without any preparation or softening of his rough edges. In the next recorded event, Jesus was eating and building relationships with Matthew's friends. These friends were desperately in need of the salvation Jesus was bringing, but they were probably a tough crowd. In fact, those in Matthew's social circle were far from the polished church crowd, but apparently, Jesus was more than willing to meet Matthew's friends where they were spiritually.

Like Matthew's friends, many teenagers are far from a reflection of Christlikeness. The process of solidifying an identity is very difficult for many teenagers. They need a place where they can be authentic and not have to pretend to be something they are not in order to find comfort. Adults must remember that like all of us, students are works in process. They will make mistakes and will be difficult to deal with at times, but our goal is to encourage authentic spiritual development, not conformity to human standards. Building relationships through fellowship that are based on unconditional love is the vehicle by which student leaders are catalysts for this type of change. Once a student leader demonstrates love and the ability to be trusted through getting to know a student well, it is more likely the student will allow that adult to know him or her more fully and affect his or her life for Christ.

Create a place where students are cared for and secure. During Jesus' reinstatement of Peter in John 21:15-19, He reminded Peter that ministry is caring for those who are in Christ. Ministry to students involves caring for them. Students do not have to look far to find circumstances in which little attention is paid to their needs. Even humanist developmental theorists like Abraham Maslow have recognized that some needs, like basic physical needs and security needs, must be met before people can devote their attention to matters of character and values. God, who designed and formed humanity, understands the intricacy of humanity's design much more than any human theorist. Within His divine plan, God has directed His people to fellowship together as an earthly picture of the care and security they experience in Him. When students are cared for and loved by godly men and women, they are more able to conceive of God's limitless love for them, and they are more likely to flourish in the security of their relationship with Christ.

Create a spirit of accountability. A third concept to recognize from Jesus' ministry to His followers is that of accountability. According to the gospel accounts, the people living in fellowship with Jesus were subject to expectations, structure, and responsibility. In the throngs of people that followed Jesus, some people were there just for the excitement or out of a hope of gaining something personally. It is unlikely that those who were present casually had much of a desire to discipline themselves to be more like Jesus or to apply His teachings. More likely, only those who truly followed Jesus with their whole lives did so within an atmosphere of accountability. Jesus loved and cared deeply for those who were committed to Him, but He also sharpened and challenged them to grow constantly.

This particular value of fellowship seems to be most difficult to apply in some student ministries. It is easy as a youth leader who loves kids to buy into the delusion that expecting too much from them will scare them away. In fact, just the opposite is likely to happen. Today's teenagers are inundated with opportunities that are tremendously exciting but completely unfulfilling. Much of the apathy seen from students probably results from the fact that they have not found anything worth committing to that is greater than their desire not to commit. When used as a tool to help students grow, accountability can benefit students by helping them understand the profit, worth, and gravity of the journey they have begun in Christ.

When called to life in Christ but not helped to live a Christlike life, many youth begin to see their faith as powerless and false instead of real and powerful. This is not to be misunderstood to say that youth ministries need to overburden teens with laws and rules. That is what the Pharisees did. It was the wrong course then, and it is the wrong course now. However, setting high expectations for students is not pharisaical. Setting high expectations for the spiritual development of students, encouraging students to grow to meet them, and dealing redemptively with their failures is part of building each other up in the context of biblical fellowship.

Create a culture of encouragement. Finally, Jesus encouraged His followers throughout the journey. In chapter 10, Luke recorded the account of Jesus sending out the 70. A careful look at the latter portion of the chapter reveals that the 70 came back excited at the ministry they perceived they had done. Jesus corrected their understanding of what had occurred. He reminded them that the power of their ministry and the resulting glory was God's, but the story does not end there. Dr. Luke recorded that, "In that same hour He rejoiced in the Holy Spirit and said, 'I praise You, Father, Lord of heaven and earth, because You have hidden these things from the wise and the learned and have revealed them to infants. Yes, Father, because this was Your good pleasure'" (Luke 10:21). Jesus acknowledged the disciples' growth and His pleasure with them. In the accountability of their relationship, He corrected them when they were wrong and taught them when they were uninformed or mistaken, but He also commended them when they grew.

How terrible it is to have a teacher and mentor who always criticizes and never acknowledges learning or good work. When His followers understood and applied His teaching, Jesus recognized it and His followers responded. They responded by building upon the thing He acknowledged. Teenagers are no different. They are constantly looking for confirmation that they are on the right track. By sincerely affirming and encouraging teenagers on a consistent basis, youth leaders have an opportunity to help teenagers cement their spiritual growth into their character and build upon it in the continuing pursuit of Christlikeness.

Biblical Keys to Fellowship

Having examined a good biblical framework from Jesus' ministry for the priorities of fellowship, we must examine the attitudes and actions that must be cultivated to see these biblical principles applied in the lives of students. Here are a few key concepts to consider:

LOVE—JOHN 13:34-35

In this passage, Jesus mandated building an atmosphere of love and acceptance within any ministry; this is particularly true in student ministry. Being an adolescent is tough because teenagers are growing and perfecting the ability to think critically about themselves and their world. That can be a scary prospect when many youth are evaluating harshly their flaws and shortcomings without a sense that anyone loves and cares for them. These teenagers feel devalued as they focus on a measure of their worth that is not God's. The kind of unconditional love modeled by Christ and demonstrated to others really resonates in the lives of growing and uncertain teenagers. Through a genuine spirit of love and acceptance that is almost nonexistent in the world at large, Christian students and adults bring glory to God and present a witness of Christ's presence in them and in the midst of their group.

ENCOURAGEMENT—1 THESSALONIANS 5:11

People, especially teenagers, can go virtually anywhere in the world to be torn down and discouraged. More and more, our culture is using the emotional "Band-Aid®" of humiliation and humor at the expense of others as a salve to treat the wounds of life. According to this passage, part of Christ-honoring fellowship among believers is intentional encouragement for others in Christ. To that end, student ministries must focus on help-

> "I give you a new commandment: that you love one another. Just as I have loved you, you should also love one another. By this all people will know that you are My disciples, if you have love for one another." (John 13:34-35)

> "Therefore encourage one another and build each other up as you are already doing" (1 Thess. 5:11).

ing students and adult leaders create a subculture of edification and encouragement that goes against the norm.

Unity—Acts 4:32-35

Unity is a clear goal for student ministry, but as we have acknowledged earlier, it is hard to achieve. Student ministers must be realistic about the unity they seek to achieve. This passage says that "the multitude of those who believed were of one heart and soul." Never have all the students in my ministry been regenerate believers. That was the goal, but a healthy student ministry has to have lost kids in it. That is part of our mission. Youth leaders must accept that real unity is a goal to be pursued but never reached for a couple of reasons. First, lost students exist outside of the fullness of unity because they are apart from Christ. While they may share in the fun and benefit of fellowship, believers' fellowship in Christ ultimately presents a witness to them of the fullness of life in Christ. Second, Christian teenagers also struggle with unity because they are immersed in a world that does not value real unity. If they have not experienced unity, they will have to be taught how to live in unity.

> "Now the multitude of those who believed were of one heart and soul, and no one said that any of his possessions was his own, but instead they held everything in common. And with great power the apostles were giving testimony to the resurrection of the Lord Jesus, and great grace was on all of them. For there was not a needy person among them, because all those who owned lands or houses sold them, brought the proceeds of the things that were sold, and laid them at the apostles' feet. This was then distributed to each person as anyone had a need" (Acts 4:32-35).

With all this discussion of unity, the age-old question of cliques is bound to surface. Does striving for unity mean driving cliques out of youth ministry? In a word, NO! Cliques are a natural part of the social development of adolescents. Developmentalists have found that most healthy adolescents need small, close-knit groups to provide a place for acquiring new social skills and for trying out adult values and social roles.[3] In plain English, that means teenagers need a circle of close friends who they can trust to give them a place to test and refine the adult behaviors and principles they are developing as they mature.

The same researchers that affirm the need for cliques also conclude that under normal circumstances multiple cliques come together to form less intimate groups known as crowds. In crowds, the members have much in common and are often similar, but they lack the closeness and trust teenagers need to feel in order to open up and be vulnerable like they need to inside their cliques. In reality, the unity youth ministers strive for within a youth group will probably more resemble a student having really close, strong relationships with a few other students in the group and having less intense but open relationships with the rest of the group. Cliques become a problem when they undermine the overall sense of unity within the ministry. When the clique is so inwardly focused or tightly closed that it begins to stand apart from the rest of your group is when there is cause for concern. In that case, adult and student leaders should take extra care to encourage the clique back toward the rest of the group. Being alert to subtle shifts in the behavior of these small groups can help youth ministry leaders encourage them back toward unified fellowship before they drift too far.

The passage in Acts 4 shows that the goal of fellowship in a healthy student ministry should be to build strong, healthy relationships among believers through the common bond in Christ. These relationships are to build up and encourage believers, to strengthen them for service in the kingdom, and to present a living picture of Christ's love to those who do not know Him. Wow! That is a lofty and complicated task. In order to approach such a complex goal, youth ministers must understand the effective tools they have at their disposal to use in meeting the goal.

Tools and Methods for Building Fellowship

A host of varied methods and activities exist as tools to foster or enhance fellowship in a student ministry. A great deal of the intentional fellowship building that takes place in a youth group is done through various forms of recreation. In his classic work, *The Ministry of Recreation,* Ray Conner defines recreation as a "freely chosen activity or experience which takes place during leisure. It has value and purpose. It generates feelings of enjoyment and satisfaction. It contributes significantly to the well-being of the individual and the community."[4] By applying the practices of recreation to the biblical function of fellowship as developed above, youth ministers unleash a powerful ministry course for four distinct reasons.

1. Recreation provides a forum for relationship building. Today's youth value relationships, but many of them lack enough significant relationships. For example, in a recent study conducted for the YMCA on parent/teen relationships, teenagers said that "not having enough time to spend together" with their parents was their top concern in life.[5] And, it's not just relationships with parents. Youth ministers can use various forms of recreation to create comfortable environments for students to form and deepen relationships with other students. They can also create opportunities for adults to begin and grow relationships with students. These relationships can ultimately earn the adult a place of significant impact in the student's life.

2. Recreation provides a means for "vicarious experience." The term *vicarious experience* is really an oxymoron, but in a world that is increasingly filled with virtual events, the value of learning through virtual experiences is understood. Recognizing the fact that junior high (and many senior high) students are very concrete in their thinking and understanding, the power of simulation and virtual experiences can be seen readily. Probably the most common example of a virtual experience in recreation is the trust fall.[6] A trust fall simulates the feeling and emotion of a faith step, and it can be used to help concrete thinking adolescents get a better understanding of an abstract concept like faith. There are literally thousands of simulation activities that can be used in recreation to support and enhance teaching done with teenagers.[7]

3. Recreation provides an opportunity to edify young believers. Playing games and engaging in fun activities allow inexperienced and often unsure youth a safe place to test knowledge they have acquired, practice skills they have learned, and build confidence in their growing abilities. These practice sessions can pay big dividends as students use their gifts and abilities to engage their culture for Christ.

4. Recreation provides time for relaxation and respite. To say the world of the average adolescent in today's society is fast-paced is a gross understatement. Part of programming for fellowship and recreation is also planning to create time for youth to rest physically and emotionally. Learning how to balance ministry activities that allow students to stop and relax with activities that push them forward is an important and needed ministry competency.

For simplicity sake, these various tools are broken down into a number of broad categories: Active recreation/sports ministry, outdoor/adventure recreation, and social recreation. Take a more detailed look at each category to discover some usable techniques for ministry.

Hints on Game Leadership

1. Plan a definite program for the time slot you have.—"Flying by the seat of your pants" can be a dangerous proposition. Always prepare a definite lineup of games, and always plan more games than you will need for the allotted time. You can always use other games later, but it is very difficult to overcome being underprepared.

2. Have the needed equipment and supplies ready for immediate use.—Dead time and needless pauses are enemies when trying to help kids to be attentive and involved in recreation. By preparing well in advance, you help your events to flow seamlessly and you help your students engage fully in the experience.

3. Keep the details of the game in mind as you explain the game.—You must be an expert on the game so you can explain it clearly. In your explanation, think of how you can answer the questions likely to be asked so you can avoid the distraction.

4. Insist on having the attention of the entire group when explaining a game.—There is not much more frustrating than having to wait through instructions to an activity over and over because someone wasn't listening. You can help the flow and pace of activities by the simple practice of insisting on students' attention before explaining a game.

Active Recreation/Sports Ministry

According to Ray Conner, "Sports and active games include any type of physical play where a team or an individual utilizes his or her skills and abilities to challenge those of his or her opponents for the purpose of competition and enjoyment, for fellowship with other persons, and for the physical exercise of the body."[8] Sports and active games are an essential part of the repertoire of any student ministry.

ACTIVE GAMES

Active games can be a great way to illustrate a point, teach a lesson, build a physical skill, or just burn off some energy. Honestly, fellowship activities built around active games or sports are not the center point of ministry they used to be, but they are one piece to the puzzle in an overall fellowship ministry strategy. When used correctly and in balance with other activities, active games can be great. Also, anyone who has ever been stranded with a bored, restless group of teenagers knows the value of knowing a few games and being able to lead them well.

SPORTS

Sports provide another vehicle for encouraging fellowship or reaching out to unsaved athletes. Many student ministries use sports leagues to provide an opportunity for students to play competitive sports in an environment that supports and encourages Christian values. Coaches who love Christ and are committed to investing time and energy into the lives of teenagers can have a powerful and lasting effect. The arena of competition can be a great place for students to "field test" much of what they learn through discipleship. Here are some things to keep in mind when planning and conducting organized sports:

1. Key in on coaches, referees, and other adult leaders who will model Christlikeness for the athletes and their families. To do this, set up a structure for training and discipling the adult leaders throughout the season.
2. Set up clearly-defined rules, policies, and procedures that support not only the integrity of the game but also the goal you have for this ministry. Once, I coached junior high boys in a church basketball league where the coach wasn't allowed to rise off the bench while the ball was in play. It was difficult, but the emphasis was on teaching and instructing players not pacing around and yelling like an NBA coach!
3. Make the Bible a part of the process. Make devotionals about life issues and prayer a part of each practice. Coaches who are well-prepared to do this and who understand the purpose of their ministry can be great disciplers.
4. Do everything with excellence. Teenagers today are accustomed to excellence in every area of life, and generally, they do not respond well to mediocrity. By maximizing the quality of your facilities, workers, and program, you communicate to students about the value of the experience.

Sports don't have to be confined to organized leagues. Impromptu games or short tournaments can be another way to weave sports into fellowship plans. Even in the most informal settings, sports can be a great way to get to know people, a great place for adults to provide a Christlike example, and a great forum for students to practice skills they are developing for effective living.

Outdoor/Adventure Recreation

Adventure recreation is a very specialized form of recreation that uses controlled risk, activity, and education in a distinctive setting. Done correctly, adventure recreation can be a powerful tool for building unity within a group and stimulating individuals to grow, discover ability, and gain confidence. Typically, adventure recreation includes a variety of group tasks or experiences designed to build trust, stimulate initiative and creative problem solving, develop healthy conflict resolution, and deal appropriately with fear and failure.

Adventure recreation moves through a fairly predictable sequence. First, leaders direct experiences in which participants discover spiritual truths through active participation in team activities like scaling a wall or negotiating a ropes course. Next, they lead the participants to understand the truths they have experienced through a debriefing process. Finally, the leaders help the participants to discover practical strategies for applying the truths they have learned. As discussed earlier, the concrete-dominated thinking processes of many adolescents lend themselves to teaching and learning through this active process, but this is not a technique you will want to use often. Part of the power in these experiences is the emotional response they create. Used too frequently, this type of recreation will lose its impact as kids become more desensitized to its stimulating effects.

Remember that while adventure recreation is a "controlled risk" activity, the risks are still very real. To use adventure recreation safely and effectively, only use facilities that insist on thorough safety procedures, well-trained personnel, and adequate bonding or insurance. Reputable facilities understand the risks they are safeguarding against and the necessity of maintaining high standards. Do not be afraid to ask for documentation that they conduct their operation safely and effectively. The safety and well-being of youth in your care are too important to be taken for granted.

Also, as a matter of course, never engage in activities that expose students to a significant risk without securing written parental permission and documents detailing student medical information and permission to seek medical attention. Accidents are accidents because they are unintentional, but you must be prepared for every contingency. While the safety of students is the primary concern, the security of your church's resources also needs to be considered. Lawsuits against churches are on the rise, and activities involving risk provide more legal exposure for your church and your personnel. It would also be worth a call to your church's insurance carrier to determine the extent of your insurance coverage and special actions or precautions that might be required in ensure your coverage. (For more hints about safety issues, see Appendix 3.)

Beware. Adventure recreation is not something a ministry should take on for itself without careful preparation. Before anyone should attempt to lead any adventure recreation activities such as high or low ropes activities, he or she should be fully trained by a certified adventure recreation trainer. Proper training is essential for safety and the proper use of these activities. Appropriate resources are also a consideration. You must have all the right equipment for any adventure element in order to ensure the safety of the element. To that end, ministries need to consider the costs involved in adventure recreation. The specialized equipment and safety gear required can be quite expensive. When considering the cost of conducting adventure recreation programs and the increased legal liability involved, most churches will find it preferable to use professional facilities with trained leaders. Christian camps and retreat centers along with some adolescent rehabilitation and treatment facilities can be good resources for adventure recreation programming.

5. Keep the rules simple and clear.—Remember this is a game, not a plan for a corporate takeover. Only give enough rules to set the structure and create an atmosphere of fair play.

6. Kill a game before it dies.—Stop playing a game while it is still fun and while your kids still want to keep playing. If you stop while they are still enjoying a game, you will be able to use the game again in the future; if you allow students to become tired of or bored with a game, it is unlikely they will ever get excited to play it again.

7. Plan activities and games in which everyone can participate.—Plan activities so that neither the highly athletic nor the highly intelligent can dominate. The best agenda of games will have opportunities for everyone to succeed.

8. Always insist on fair play.—Model the virtues of truth and fairness even in the small things.

9. Be open to adapt and modify games.—Do not be afraid to make a good thing better. Take favorite games and add twists or new elements to make them new again.

10. Laughter at someone else's expense is always in poor taste.—*This is an axiom that may have been long in coming in youth ministry. If you can imagine, there was a day when many of the "fun" resources available to youth ministers promoted humiliation or embarrassment of students as a way to have fun. Forget it. We want to minister to students who hurt and build them up not tear them down.*

11. Where there is action, there are accidents.—*Physical activity means accidents (and yes, injuries) will inevitably occur. The chief concern here is to prepare and conduct yourself so you eliminate as many potential accidents as possible and to prepare yourself adequately to respond effectively when accidents occur.*

These tips are adapted from the work of Dr. Jim Minton, who currently serves as Professor of Psychology at the University of Mobile in Mobile, Alabama.

Social Recreation

Social recreation is perhaps the most common and consistently used form of fellowship programming in student ministry. Social recreation can be any type of occasion that involves people interacting with other people. These occasions can be anything from a structured banquet or a themed fellowship to informal and less-structured events like a coffee house or a picnic. Social recreation provides the opportunity for people to meet new people and build relationships with them and for those who are already acquainted to grow their relationships deeper. It would be impossible to deal exhaustively with all of the creative ways student ministers have found to use social recreation, but here are a few general fellowship types and some ideas for their use.

THEMED FELLOWSHIPS

After-church or other occasional fellowships have long been a mainstay of local church ministry to teenagers particularly for churches in rural settings. The busyness of life, the difficulty of exciting kids who seem to have seen everything, and the desire of kids to just "hang out" with each other have all come together to render the concept of youth fellowship passé in the minds of many student ministers. True, fellowships may not be the one-size-fits-all, multi-functional ministry tool they were decades ago, but they are a viable ministry programming element. Regular scheduling of fellowships provides an opportunity for students to have fun in the context of Christian nurture, to learn skills for life—like learning to relate to other people, and to experience other people in a relaxed environment.

Consider what makes a good fellowship:

1. **Select an attractive theme.**—Fellowships are meant to be enjoyable. Creative ideas and exciting themes add to the enjoyment. If you have trouble gauging what might be appealing to your students, ask them. Putting together fellowship ideas can be a great job for a lead team or a student advisory group.[9] The calendar can be a great ally in fellowship planning. Fellowships planned around a theme drawn from holiday seasons or cultural happenings, such as the Super Bowl, can capitalize on the attention already being paid to the time of year and can create a synergy of excitement for your event. Also, when planning a theme, consider the possible promotional alternatives for the theme. For instance, say you plan for an after-church fellowship on Super Bowl Sunday. You decide to call it the "Souper Bowl" and center the theme on football-related games and serve homemade soups for food. For promotion, you could include plastic spoons and disposable bibs in a mailed flyer to advertise the event. While this might sound corny, your objective is to raise consciousness and curiosity about your event so students will want to be there to be a part of the action. Above all, do not be afraid to be creative. Quirky ideas can be genius if they tap into the imagination of your students. Just be careful your creativity does not go completely unchecked. Before you launch out in an edgy direction for a fellowship theme, consider how people inside and outside your church might receive it and respond to it. You can save yourself much grief by avoiding misunderstandings before they occur.

Basic Student Ministry

2. **Plan a schedule that works.**—For a two- or three-hour gathering, pacing is key. Make sure the time is structured enough to eliminate boredom, but be careful not to push kids through an experience like a drill sergeant. Thoughtful planning far enough in advance will allow for construction of a fellowship experience with elements that work together to promote a spirit of fun and community. For a two-hour fellowship, consider a schedule like this:

   - *Arrival activities (20 min.)*—Plan some activities that get kids involved as soon as they arrive. Use mixer games to help them get acquainted, thinking games that help introduce them to one another, or whatever else will get them into the flow of the experience from the beginning. These activities should also be designed to provide some flexible time for late arrivals and so forth.
   - *Games/activities (30 min.)*—Plan games and activities that work well together. Ideally, you want a pace that will allow you to move as seamlessly as possible from one activity to another. Idle hands might not always be the devil's workshop, but bored students are the student minister's nightmare. If students are not engaged in the experience you have created, they will find ways to amuse themselves. Often their amusement can be at the expense of someone or something you would rather they leave alone. Good pacing gives them less opportunity to wander mentally or physically in ways that might be unacceptable. Prepared and participating adult leaders are the key to smooth functioning. If one individual is trying to do everything, it will be virtually impossible to maintain a healthy pace. Also, don't forget to plan too much to do for the time you have allotted. Overplanning will permit you to end activities that are not working and still have something ready to go without worrying about running out of activities. Remember, you can always use the extra activities later. Finally, in planning activities, remember the "Hints on Game Leadership." (See Minton's sidebar.)
   - *Refreshments (15 min.)*—There are two things to remember here. First, metabolically speaking, kids have much faster running engines than most adults. Translated, that means many of them are hungry and thirsty often (especially when they are active). This means you need to stop for food and drinks fairly often. Hungry kids will rapidly become frustrated and cranky kids, so do not spare the refreshments. Second, kids do not need much time to eat. While adults may like to linger over a snack and enjoy it, most kids just want to get food consumed and get back to the action. A fellowship is not the time to compromise on eating time. Concentrate on foods that can be served fast, eaten fast, and cleaned up fast.
   - *More games/activities (30 min.)*—Follow the same suggestions as before, but consider bringing down the activity level if a devotional or spiritual emphasis is intended as a part of the fellowship.
   - *Refreshments (10 min.)*—Give them another refueling opportunity before you move on.
   - *Spiritual emphasis/free time (15 min.)*—If you choose to have a teaching time or devotional moment, it is a great idea to use the activity of the fellowship as a tie-in to the concept you are teaching. You may decide the fellowship you have built is an end in itself. If so, consider some free time to talk and play as an ending point.

3. **Promote the event.**—Good advertising builds interest. Promote the event by making sure parents and students know who, what, when, where, and why about the event through a variety of communication channels. Some prefer information communi-

cated verbally, while others are attracted by visually interesting promotion. Use both. Use them creatively and use them often. Overcommunication is to be preferred as opposed to undercommunication.

4. **Gather materials and prepare for the event.**—The work put into preparation will find its reward in a smooth running fellowship that meets the goal of adding to the fellowship of the group. Here are several tips for preparation:

- Once you have a fellowship plan, make out a detailed list of all the equipment, supplies, and food necessary for the size group you expect to attend. Advanced planning increases the chance that all the supplies necessary can be located, and it increases the opportunity to include others in ministry service through the delegation of tasks.

- Delegation also applies to adult leaders who will be facilitating the fellowship. It is a good idea to meet with the leaders at least several days before the fellowship to review the fellowship plan and delegate work assignments.

When selecting adults, remember you can pull in just about anyone to stand by and watch. You need people who will actively participate in leadership. Consider staffing with the following adult roles:

Greeters—Have some adults or student leaders on hand to greet people as they arrive and help them get involved in the arrival activities.

Activity Leader—Someone who is both well-acquainted with the fellowship plan and all its elements and possesses the ability to communicate effectively with students should be given the responsibility to direct the activity of the fellowship like a master of ceremonies. The activity leaders should be able to explain the games, officiate (if necessary), and direct the flow of the fellowship.

Active Participants—Some adults can plan to be involved in the games/activities with the students. Because they know what is planned in advance, they can help students understand the activities, and they can be a source of excitement in the process. For this task, choose leaders that will not be shy to dive into the activities fully. These adults will set the tone. They will also get some great interaction time with the students.

Advanced Activity Leaders—A couple of adults can work one step ahead of the action by preparing for the next activity while the current activity is still occurring. This will allow the activity leader to concentrate on the activity at hand and still be able to move quickly to the next fellowship element.

Refreshment Delegates—Several people could be put in charge of preparing refreshments and have them ready at the appropriate time.

Safety Workers—Several adults should be given the sole responsibility of inspecting the fellowship area for safety before the event. During the activities, these same workers should continue to monitor the area for possible safety problems and work in the activity to keep participants safe (for example, to keep blindfolded game participants from running into a wall). Please see Appendix 3 entitled Safety and Legal Issues for more information.

Basic Student Ministry

5. **Conduct the event.**—With all of the preparation that has been put into the event, be confident and work your plan.
6. **Evaluate the event.**—Improvement requires honest evaluation of past efforts to discover things worth repeating, things needing correcting, and things for renouncing. Gather input from students, parents, and youth workers as you evaluate. Also, keep good notes and records of the planning process and include written notes of your after-fellowship evaluation with these records when the fellowship is complete. Keeping a file of this information will make it easier to reference in future fellowship planning.

SPECIAL EVENTS

There are all kinds of special events that give youth groups a chance to fellowship. Planning fellowship opportunities around school events can be great. Tailgating before a game or a fifth quarter fellowship after a game are ways to link up fellowship to events that will already attract a number of students. Lock-ins can be another great special event fellowship. Because you have a great deal of contact with students compressed into a short time period, you can actually accomplish multiple objectives during a lock-in (evangelism, discipleship, worship, or ministry), but they also provide a great forum for fellowship and relationship-building with students both inside and on the fringes of your ministry.

COFFEE HOUSES

As said before, many student ministers have noted the trend among teenagers to just want to "hang out." While activity-based fellowships are still working well for some youth groups, others have almost given up on them because their kids would rather just spend time talking and relating to each other. In this circumstance, games and organized events just seem to get in the way. A ministry approach that seems to work can be drawn from the coffee house concept that became popular in the 1960s. Coffee houses have been around forever, but they still work. The idea is pretty simple. Allocate a space where kids can come, see each other, talk, meet new people, and generally just socialize. Throw in some food, comfortable places to sit, plenty of room to mingle, some background music, and "Voilá!" You have yourself a coffee house (and you do not even have to serve coffee).

You can tailor the environment to suit your group by using things like live musical performances, games (such as ping pong or video games), or other touches, but the principle idea is just a safe place to gather and enjoy relationships. These events are also a great way for adult leaders to spend time with students and get to know them better. Adults can become a part of the mingling and visiting mix to get some quality time with students, but remember that when adults venture around in a setting like this, they are venturing onto the teenager's turf. Adults need to concentrate on relationship-building and getting to know students, not impressing them. Earning the right to be heard by a student comes through relationship.

MEALS

Fellowship and food seem to go together like peanut butter and jelly! We only need go back to the Old Testament feasts or the New Testament practice of a fellowship meal in conjunction with the Lord's Supper to see the connection between eating and the fellowship of God's people. In fellowship, food can either be part of the plan or it can be the main attraction. Banquets are a

---

BIRTHDAY FELLOWSHIPS

Birthdays are a great opportunity for fellowship with students. Plan a monthly fellowship with all of the students who have a birthday that month. Provide a cake and all the trimmings, just like a normal birthday party. These fellowships also bring together some interesting mixes of students that might not otherwise spend time with each other. In larger ministries, birthday fellowships could be used by Sunday School departments or other groups within the group. The point is to let students know that their birthdays are a big deal to you. Any opportunity to take a personal interest in the life of a student can open the door for a deeper relationship. When they know you love them, you earn the right to minister to them.

—Mark Pendergrass, minister to youth, Brookwood Baptist Church, Birmingham, Alabama

great way to use meals in fellowship. Whether it's a '50s banquet with adult servers on roller skates (make sure your insurance in paid up!) or an international meal with a missions flair, a banquet can be a special occasion to share food, conversation, and fun. Consider some of the following banquet/meal variations to use for fellowship:

- Sweetheart Banquet
- Hawaiian Luau
- Progressive Dinner (each course of the meal in a different location)
- Family meals (Invite small groups of students to the homes of youth leaders for an old-fashioned family-style meal complete with conversation around the table.)
- Picnics
- Holiday meals
- Recognition banquets
- Graduation banquets
- Sports banquets (Host sports teams from the local high school for a banquet and celebration at the end of the season.)

FAMILY FELLOWSHIPS

With all the attention churches place on the need for strong families, often church programming seems to undermine that value. Think about it. More and more, typical church programming is sending every member of the family in a different direction at every turn. Fellowship programming can be a great way to minister to families by putting them together. Phil Briggs said it best when he said, "Fellowships between parents and youth will strengthen the bond between the different age groups. Teenagers estranged from their parents see their peers and parents relating, and parents see other adults relating to their child. Both generations gain a broader, healthier perspective on each other. If the events are well-planned and publicized, they can result in unifying a group of youth with the parents."[10]

Look for some natural connection points to bring parents and their children together. For example, picnics on Labor Day, Memorial Day, or the Fourth of July can take advantage of time when parents and students are both available. Consider altering the student ministry calendar to reinvent some existing events as family events. Many fellowships, retreats, and other activities could be restructured to include parents. Not everything should have a family twist, but it is a healthy goal to get families together for enjoyment and to build them up.

INTERGENERATIONAL FELLOWSHIPS

Students falling away from active involvement in church after they graduate from high school is not a new problem. Intergenerational fellowship could be one step in helping students remain an active part of the body of Christ after they leave the youth group. Typically, churched teenagers have a variety of specialized programming that separates them from the church as a whole. At a minimum, most youth groups have their own discipleship, fellowship, and ministry programming that exists separately (or alongside) the mainstream of the church. In some cases, student ministries exist almost totally apart from the rest of the church, accomplishing all of the functions of the church by themselves without much meaningful interaction with the rest of the church. Is it any wonder students nurtured in this environment leave the church when they graduate from the student ministry? They are forced to move out into an unfamiliar church world where they may

Basic Student Ministry

have few meaningful relationships. If you add the generational barriers that may be perceived to exist, many young adults drift away to find places to spend their time where they are more comfortable.

By creating opportunities for youth to fellowship with the other age groups in the church on a regular basis, teenagers can become an integral part of the church. Fellowship can build a bridge of understanding and connect teenagers to the entire local body of believers in a way that will nurture them long after their youth group years. One of the most beneficial connections that can be made in a church is the one between teenagers and senior adults. While many student ministries find difficulty helping youth and senior adults coexist in the church, conflict does not have to exist. In fact, looking at the life assets and needs of each group, no two groups in the church are positioned to have a more beneficial relationship. If you can get both groups to get past issues of dress, music, and slang, they actually are very compatible. With some work, student ministries can partner with senior adults to create the type of church community called for in Scripture. To foster intergenerational fellowship with senior adults, consider the following:

- Enlist senior adults to pray for specific students during trips like a youth camp or a mission trip. After the trip, plan a social gathering for the students to share with their senior prayer partners what God accomplished in their lives during the trip.
- Consider leading senior adults to invite small groups of students to come to their homes for home-cooked meals.
- Challenge senior adults to serve as stand-in parents for students whose parents are not involved at special church events.
- Encourage students to adopt "grandparents" from the senior adult ministry.

Intergenerational fellowship does not need to be created just with the oldest group in the church. Look for opportunities to encourage interaction and relationship building between teenagers and all of the age groups in the church.

Fellowship and MAP

Fellowship in Open Groups

Fellowship is an integral part of the strategy of open groups. As you have read earlier, open groups are open to any student at any time, and they have an intentional evangelistic focus. Building fellowship within the open group will serve to strengthen students already a part of the group and to enhance the evangelistic appeal to students the group is trying to reach. Many of the strategies already identified as effective for the entire youth group can be equally effective on a smaller scale with an open group. Open groups like Sunday school classes or cell groups provide an opportunity for adults to focus on building significant relationships with a small group of students. Truly, the effectiveness of an adult's teaching and modeling with a student is proportional to the investment the adult is willing to make in the life of the student.

Outreach and personal contact outside of the classroom experience have long been part of the successful open group formula, and there is no reason to think it will change. Personal investments should also be encouraged from one student to another. Giving students responsibility for contacting, praying for, and ministering to their classmates can go a long way to building group unity. Open group fellowship should be open to all students who could appropriately be a part of the group. Here are a handful of ideas for fellowship with an open group:

A strategy for biblical fellowship can be achieved through and open group program. An open group where students can come together to build relationships with one another and adults is a great place for biblical fellowship to occur. In our open groups, we strive to accomplish what can be called, "Building relationships around God's Word." The phrase gives a mental picture of open groups focused on biblical fellowship. After being exposed to a Scriptural truth, students move to discuss the truth and see how it applies to their lives. Picture a small group of teens and a youth leader sitting in a circle talking about Scripture, sharing about the issues of life with the Bible—metaphorically and literally—in the center of the circle as the basis for their discussion and thus their fellowship. Through this discussion and application of the truth, they began to learn about each other—their life situations, strengths and struggles, beliefs, prayer needs, and so on. This weekly time also provides a foundation for further relationship-building and fellowship through the week. All of this accomplished through an open group program, focused on fellowship (biblical fellowship), and "relationships built around God's Word."
—Jason Stewart
associate minister to students
FBC, Cleveland, Tennessee

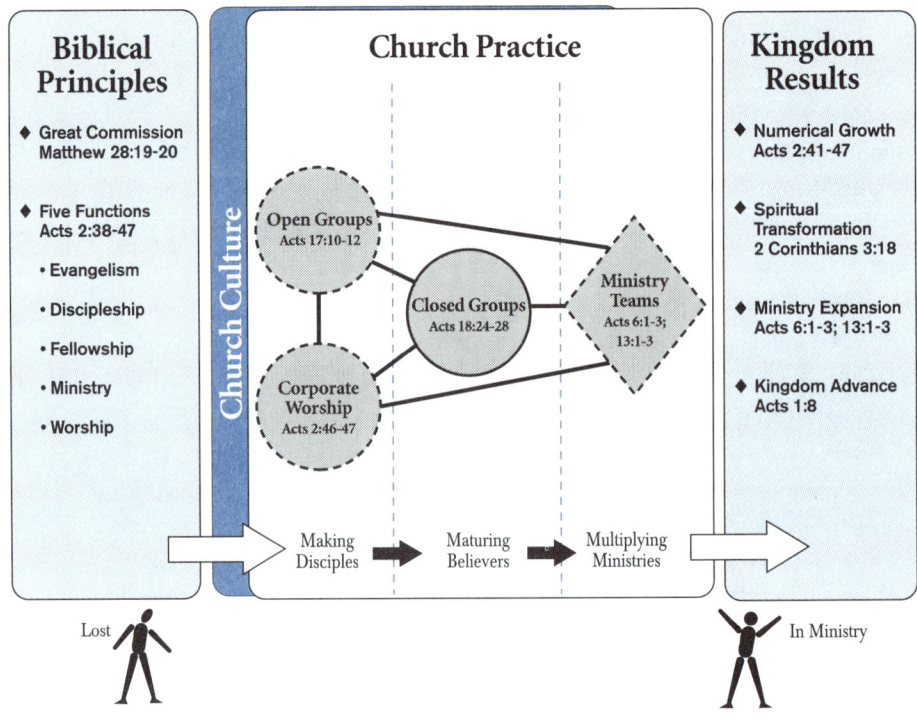

A Kingdom-Focused Church Model and Process

- Have lunch as a group
- Attend a sporting event together
- Complete a ministry project
- Decorate your meeting room
- See an appropriate movie
- Hold a game night at a member's house

If your group holds all its small groups in one location at the same time, another idea would be to have some time set aside before the teaching time begins to mingle and talk over some light refreshments. The social time might also help the teaching time that follows by allowing students to visit before class instead of during class.

FELLOWSHIP IN CLOSED GROUPS

Fellowship among members of a closed group is crucial. In closed discipleship groups, intimacy is essential if students are to benefit fully from the experience. Students and adults in closed groups can build a bond of trust that will carry over into their ability to dig deep into the Word and into each other's lives. Only by spending significant time together can students feel comfortable opening themselves up to each other. It is a gradual, progressive process. Because fellowship should be such a consistent part of the closed group process, you might consider making regular fellowship time a part of the design of the group structure.

FELLOWSHIP AND CORPORATE WORSHIP

In a sense, worship is in part the vertical expression of fellowship—our fellowship with God. In His Word, God has linked worship with fellowship. In Matthew 5:23-24, Jesus instructed believers to be reconciled to a brother who has something against them before they are to worship Him through giving. True worship is predicated on right fellowship, and we need to teach students accordingly. Many students love to sing praises and to worship, but they need to be instructed that how they live with others has an impact on the worth of their worship. Teaching on themes of forgiveness, reconciliation, and conflict resolution are essential to both fellowship and worship.

Fellowship and Ministry Teams

As presented earlier, almost any fellowship gathering in student ministry can be accomplished by a ministry team. Getting students, parents, and youth workers involved in building fellowship for the youth group will also build fellowship for the ministry team. Teams working together toward a common goal can create strong and healthy relationships that will bolster the overall fellowship of your group.

Discipline

A discussion concerning fellowship and teenagers would be incomplete without reference to some issues related to discipline. Discipline can be one of the most daunting tasks for a student ministry to address. Discipline is not just to keep order. It is to help students to learn to practice self-discipline by using external constraints to help guide them. While there is no magic formula for discipline, here are a few suggestions:[11]

1. **Work on relationships first.**—Similar to the previous discussion about accountability, authentic relationships will help you to get a good result when you have to exercise discipline with a teenager. If they trust you and your care for them, they are more likely to follow your correction.
2. **Seek to understand individual youth.**—No two teenagers are alike, and we should seek to understand them individually. We should also seek to discipline them appropriately based upon their unique personalities and circumstances.
3. **Let youth be youth.**—Expecting youth to act like adults is unrealistic. Sometimes they will be loud, spirited, or sidetracked, but that is to be expected.
4. **Make the guidelines clear.**—A clear understanding of the expectations is vital for good discipline. Make sure that students understand why the guidelines exist and allow them to participate in the establishment of the guidelines. Students will support things in which they have ownership. When the guidelines are theirs too, they are more likely to buy into them. Also, expect students to live within the guidelines. Positive expectations will go a long way to creating an atmosphere where students are comfortable within the limits.
5. **Be sure the consequence fits the crime.**—Setting the consequences up front will help keep you from overreacting and help kids understand the things that are out of bounds. Also, when you have to discipline a student, it will not seem arbitrary.

Conclusion

The clear biblical mandate for student ministry is to cultivate fellowship that brings students and adults together under their common bond in Christ. Fellowship is one of God's eternal purposes for the church—no body of believers is complete without fellowship. According to the Scripture, there are some actions youth ministers can teach, model, and encourage that will promote fellowship.

Fellowship has an intentional purpose and a rightful place in student ministry programming. Because fellowship is a purpose of the church, it is a purpose of the student ministry. In one sense, fellowship is encouraged within a group because groups mirror the church. In another sense, fellowship is encouraged with the rest of the church because groups are part of the larger body of believers. Fellowship with the entire church should never be forgotten as an ongoing priority.

Fellowship is more than fun and games, but recreation can be a powerful part of an overall fellowship strategy. Recreation provides a healthy forum for building fellowship. Whether active recreation like games or adventure activities or social gatherings like a meal, recreation is a vehicle that works, but it is only one part of a complete fellowship strategy.

The challenge for student ministry leaders is to use the available ministry tools to set the conditions where fellowship is likely to happen. Not every group of students will respond to the same type of fellowship programming. Feel the freedom to design fellowship ministries that minister to your students. Just because someone else has been successful with an idea doesn't mean it is for you, and just because an idea has never been tried doesn't mean it will not work. Use the knowledge you have developed of your students and your community along with the creativity with which God has blessed you and others around you!

---

[1] For more information on the history of youth ministry see Mark Senter III, *The Coming Revolution in Youth Ministry and Its Radical Impact on the Church* (Wheaton: Victor, 1992), and Merton Strommen "A Recent Invention: The Profession of Youth Ministry" in Merton Strommen, Karen Jones, and Dave Rahn, *Youth Ministry That Transforms: A comprehensive analysis of the hopes, fears, and effectiveness of today's youth workers* (Grand Rapids: Zondervan, 2001).

[2] See Doug Fields, *Purpose Driven Youth Ministry: 9 Essential Foundations for Healthy Growth* (Grand Rapids: Zondervan, 1998).

[3] Laura E. Berk, *Development Through the Lifespan* (2nd ed.) (Boston: Allyn and Bacon, 2002), 404-5.

[4] Ray Conner, *The Ministry of Recreation* (Nashville: Convention Press, 1992), 24.

[5] Global Youth Strategy Group, "Talking with Teens: The YMCA Parent and Teen Survey Final Report." [Cited 10 November 2002] Available from the Internet: *www.ymca.net/presrm/research/teensurvey*.

[6] A trust fall involves having a subject fall backward off of an elevated platform into the waiting arms of a group of people who will catch them and prevent them from hitting the ground.

[7] For a good starting point see *The Centrifuge Games CD* (Nashville: LifeWay Press, 2002).

[8] Conner, 88.

[9] For more information on lead teams see chapter 6.

[10] Phil Briggs, "Parent/Youth Recreation" in Diana Garland, et.al. *Life Changing Events for Youth and Their Families* (Nashville: Convention Press, 1995), 62.

[11] Adapted from Allen Jackson and Randy Johnson, *Connected, Committed, and a Little Bit Crazy: Teaching Youth the Bible* (Nashville: Convention Press, 1996), 107.

chapter 4

MINISTRY

Allen Jackson

> *Ministry grows out of a transformed and serving life. Ministry is meeting another person's need in the name of Jesus, expressed as service to persons inside the church family and expressed as missions to persons outside the church.*
> —Gene Mims, Vice President LifeWay Church Resources

"I'M JUST NOT INTO, LIKE, ORGANIZED religion—going to church and sitting there trying to listen. I like to do stuff—we did a Habitat for Humanity project once as a youth group. It was awesome to see the look on the lady's face when we finished her roof.

—*Colin, 15*
New Orleans, Louisiana

I am looking at a brochure from days gone by that has as its heading (as have a number of pamphlets from a number of different organizations), "What Is Youth Ministry?" The subject for this chapter is "ministry," so for starters it would be good to come to grips with some terms. "Youth Ministry" as the generic title for a vocation is different from "ministry" which is part of the model described in this book. In this chapter, when I speak of "youth ministry," I am referring to the program. When I talk about "ministry," I am thinking of a specific purpose or specific actions within the context of the youth program.

> **"Whoever wants to become great among you must be your servant, and whoever wants to be first among you must be your slave; just as the Son of Man did not come to be served but to serve and give His life–a ransom for many" (Matt. 20:26b-28).**

Youth Ministry Defined

When I asked around my office for a definition of *youth ministry,* folks looked at each other like it was one of those definitions that is so well-known that we take for granted that we know what it is. Nobody defines water. We just drink it, cook with it, wash cars with it, swim in it. We don't try to agree on a specific definition unless we are scientists or water filter salesmen.

So it is with youth ministry. After all, we are in the business of ministry with teenagers and maybe there is a definition somewhere that sounds like a youth group mission statement. Commonly acknowledged, youth ministry is what we as adults do to be Jesus to teenagers. Instinctively, we understand we are missionaries to the youth culture. Perhaps the sentiment was captured by my assistant who said, "It is working with kids for God."

Youth ministry happens when, as Mark Senter said, "A Christian adult finds a comfortable method of entering a student's world."[1] It is incarnational. In a very real sense, persons who work with youth (whether paid or volunteer) model the theological truth we call incarnation. Even as Jesus inserted Himself into the world of humanity, so adults insert themselves (sacrificially) into the world of students. Jesus came into our world and became one of us. Adults who work with youth enter the youth culture. Jim Rayburn, the founder of Young Life, was one of the first to emphasize the incarnational ministry of Jesus as a foundation in youth ministry. Warren Benson, describing Rayburn's methodology, wrote:

> Wise youth workers go where high school people are, as Jesus did. The incarnational nomenclature projects an analogy of what God accomplished in the person of His Son. In Jesus, God came down to us, became one of us, and identified with us, even though we were separated from Him because of the impasse of our sin. Christ's substitutionary atonement made it possible for us to be reconciled with the Father and have the impasse removed.[2]

The analogy can be taken too far. Adults can be only the messengers of redemption, not the providers of atonement. It also breaks down if we try to insist that adults need to be youth. Far too many adults look foolish trying to imitate adolescents. Nonetheless, ministry with youth means being in their world and in their lives.

As Richard Ross ably captures in his chapter on administration, we need to be strategic about how we put feet to the incarnational attitude via the local church youth ministry program. Many youth ministers have done extremely well describing the intent or purpose—the "how" of youth ministry. For example, consider a part of a stated youth ministry strategy. Randy Fields, in his online article, described the intentionality of the youth ministry at his church.

Our church has identified some crucial elements in a well-rounded youth ministry . . . Our basic philosophy is this:
- *To have and build a dynamic relationship with God and His Word.*
- *To have and build a dynamic relationship with fellow believers.*
- *To have and build a dynamic relationship with nonbelievers and share the love of Christ with them.*

How we live out the philosophy is identified by successive steps up the ladder. Each step must be completed before the next step:
- *Step 1: Come and See*
- *Step 2: Commitment*
- *Step 3: Growth*
- *Step 4: Personal Ministry*
- *Step 5: Ministry Above and Beyond*[3]

I think Randy has done an excellent job describing an intended flow for students as they attach themselves to the ministry. In the MAP diagram, the desired movement is from "Lost" to "In Ministry" (making disciples to multiplying disciples). In chapter 2, we identified four levels of student commitment. The desire is to lead students to step up in their commitment level and help them to move from a "beginning" level of spiritual maturity, to a "basic" level, and finally to an "advanced" level. "Crowd" students are teenagers who live or move within a particular locale. "Group" students are students who have responded to an invitation and who have attended a youth ministry event at least once. "Committed" and "Multiplier" students are at church because they want to be. (See chapter 2.)

Given a general definition of youth ministry, acknowledging the incarnational nature, and committing to intentional design, we are now confronted with the ministry context of current youth culture. While the emphasis on relationships between caring adults and students remains, youth culture has not stayed the same. The environment in which we do youth ministry has morphed dramatically. (See sidebar.)

Youth Ministry: Still Relationships

In spite of the technological changes, ministry with teenagers is still about relationships. Programmatically, youth ministry in a local church is generally considered to be all of the activities scheduled on behalf of youth in junior and senior high school. (See the definition in the introduction.) It is the generic term to describe the program or the diet of events a church might sponsor on behalf of those students generally between seventh grade until (and sometimes beyond) high school graduation. LifeWay defines youth ministry as the ministry targeting youth from grades 7–12. In some cases, sixth graders may actually be a part of a church's youth ministry. For developmental reasons, however, it is probably best to classify sixth graders as a unique subset to be addressed through the children's ministry.

Youth ministry has been described as both a historical concept and a 20th century invention. Merton Strommen traced concern for youth back to Martin Luther's address to the precursors of the juvenile justice system in Germany: "I pray all of you for the sake of God and of youth, not to think slightly of educational problems. For it is a serious matter, at the heart of Christ and all mankind that we help and advise the young people."[4]

The 20th century accelerated the birth of local church and parachurch youth ministries with a social climate that separated adolescents from adults and children and made them

---

At past camps we would gather contraband in the form of candy or food. Now we are forced to consider cabin searches for all manner of illegal items. We used to make jokes about the "What to Bring/What Not to Bring" list. We just updated it to try to consider what to do with MP3 players, CD players, palmtop computers. PDA no longer means "public display of affection," but now encompasses personal digital assistants or Palm Pilots®.

On bus trips we used to think in terms of the value of Walkmans®. Now we find that X-boxes®, Playstations®, and Game Cubes® fill suitcases. A few years ago, we were worried and concerned about what movies to show on the bus ride up on the "fancy" TV/VCR system on the state-of-the-art charter bus. This year, we have students bringing their own laptops and/or personal DVD players. Don't worry about students sneaking out to a movie because most students carry DVD players and numerous movies with them. As technology has increased at such a rapid rate, the prices for electronics have gone the opposite direction. What was unaffordable last year is feasible this year for the average teenager with a part-time job.

With the incredible ease to stay connected, parents and the church know more about what is going on during the youth retreat than the youth pastor leading the event. Johnny calls home to talk to mommy on his cell phone and tells her that his friend Bobby had a little practical joke played on him. The next day the rumor that had begun to spread around the church at home was that Bobby had been harassed by the older boys on the trip (when actually it was his friends playing around together and he was fine). But, Bobby's mom is on the way to get him and you don't even know. The office staff at the church and parents seem to know more than the student pastor and often he is surprised by their comments concerning what has happened.

Just a couple of years ago the youth ministry rebellion act was a water balloon here or a pillow fight there. Now, students are swinging from the rafters practically naked, pulling pranks on other students. Thus, the issue of secular students crash with today's heightened sense of harassment issues.
—Melvin Swafford, FBC Cleveland, Tennessee

a social class unto themselves. Adolescence, defined in my classes as "that period of time between puberty and the acceptance of adult responsibility," has lengthened with earlier puberty and later responsibility. When schools, industry, and the judicial system began to see adolescents as in between childhood and adulthood, ministries followed. As early as 1881, the Christian Endeavor society was instituted by Frances Clark (parachurch) while local church youth ministry has been traced back as far as 1859 with Dwight L. Moody's Sunday School class[5] or 1937 when the Third Baptist Church of St. Louis, Missouri, called a full-time "youth director," the first known staffing by a Southern Baptist Church.[6] But enough background, what is ministry within youth ministry?

The Difference Between Youth Ministry and Doing Ministry

So what is the difference between youth ministry and youth "doing" ministry? The "ministry" described here is not the comprehensive youth program in a local church or community described above. "Ministry" for the current discussion is comprised of two things. First, it is one of the functions of youth ministry, and therefore a chapter heading in this book. Second, it is the part of the youth program that involves activities undertaken by students and adult volunteers intending, in part, to turn the focus outward *from* the church and *to* the community (mission) but also to meet needs of the group within the church body as well (service).

Ministry as a Function

The functions of youth ministry are generally accepted to be evangelism, discipleship, fellowship, ministry, and worship. Doug Fields extracted these from the Bible passages known as the Great Commandment:

> He said to him, " 'You shall love the Lord your God with all your heart, with all your soul, and with all your mind.' This is the greatest and most important commandment. The second is like it: 'You shall love your neighbor as yourself.' All the Law and the Prophets depend on these two commandments." Matthew 22:37-40

and the Great Commission:

> "Go, therefore, and make disciples of all nations, baptizing them in the name of the Father and of the Son and of the Holy Spirit, teaching them to observe everything I have commanded you. And remember, I am with you always, to the end of the age." Matthew 28:19-20

Fields suggested, The five functions are found in these two passages:[7]
- Worship: "Love the Lord your God with all your heart"
- Ministry: "Love your neighbor as yourself"
- Evangelism: "Go and make disciples"
- Fellowship: "Baptizing them"
- Discipleship: "Teaching them to obey"

These five functions form the backbone of this book. All are necessary in order for a youth ministry in a local church to be balanced and holistic. Ministry as a function is an assumption that the good news cannot be kept within the church, and that students will only mature by being obedient to the Great Commandment and the Great Commission. Gene Mims defined ministry as a function as, "meeting another person's need in Christ's name."[8] Fields defined it as, "meeting needs with love." Fields elaborated,

> In youth ministry we need to clearly communicate that these God-given gifts don't come with an age limitation. Students shouldn't have to wait until they are adults to minister. A healthy youth ministry will constantly encourage students to discover their gifts and put them into practice through ministry and mission opportunities. When the purpose (function) of ministry is applied, you will graduate student ministers rather than program attendees.[9]

In his classic work, *New Testament Theology*, Frank Stagg (citing T.W. Manson) concerning the *ministry* (emphasis mine) of the church:

> There is only one "essential ministry in the Church, the perpetual ministry of the risen and ever-present Lord Himself." That is, Jesus the Christ—who ministered in Judea, Samaria, and Galilee—continues His ministry through His church, His body. It is He who preaches in all true preaching; it is He who teaches, heals, comforts, judges, directs. All other ministries within the church are derived from, and dependent upon, that of the living Lord Jesus.[10]

The ministry of the church and of the youth ministry is an extension of the ministry of Jesus. The now tired phrase "what would Jesus do?" is appropriate to use as a measure of the ministry among teenagers in our churches. The very concept of youth ministry is an extension of the ministry of Christ. Every program, fellowship, camp, DiscipleNow, and mission trip should be placed under the scrutiny of that concept. Does each of these activities extend the ministry of Christ or advance the kingdom of God?

The constant question to ask is the ministry question, Do these things extend the ministry of Jesus (i.e. proclaiming the kingdom, healing the sick, showing compassion for the downtrodden, building up the saints, teaching, serving others)? Again quoting Stagg,

> There is no provision for a non-ministering church or for non-ministering members. The idea of "drones" or non-working Christians is foreign to the New Testament idea of the church. To be in the body of Christ is to be a part of His working body.[11]

Ministry is meeting another person's need in the name of Jesus, expressed as service to persons inside the church family and expressed as missions to persons outside the church.[11] Unfortunately many of our ministries solely are inwardly-focused, arguably producing more knowledgeable disciples, but probably not more effective ones. My favorite illustration is that of a hydroelectric plant that produces just enough electricity to keep the lights on in the plant. Much, if not most, of the activity called ministry is reinvested into the members of the youth ministry.

A dynamic tension exists in youth ministry between evangelism, discipleship, and ministry (keeping with the definition of ministry as outwardly-focused actions). Evangelism is the act of proclaiming the gospel and asking for a response. Discipleship is the equipping of the saints for ministry. Ministry is the missions action of a church on behalf of the poor, the oppressed, or the community at large and service to and within the body of Christ. It is evident that a balanced youth ministry must include all three. Imagine a three-legged stool with legs of evangelism, discipleship, and ministry. With one leg, you could

He has told you, O man, what is good. And what does the Lord require of you other than to act justly, to love faithfulness, and to walk carefully with your God (Micah 6:8).

lean, with two legs you could prop, but all three legs are needed in order for the stool to do what it was designed to do—hold all of your weight.

John Stott, said "Social involvement was both the child of evangelical religion and the twin sister of evangelism,"[12] and that, "social activity was said to be…a bridge to evangelism, and indeed the two were declared to be partners. Besides, they are united by the gospel."[13] Some youth ministers may feel they are not "gifted" in one of the three areas. As Fields indicated, an accurate understanding of the words of Jesus that we call the Great Commission clearly indicates a balance of the three is holistic and faithful ministry.

Many scholars render the English imperative, *go* to read literally, *as you are going*, to indicate that going is what Christians do. Making disciples and teaching (ministry) is what they do as they go. Biblically, ministry is always the by-product of obedience (as you are going). In the Old Testament Book of Micah (6:8), the prophet linked the output of ministry as the by-product of an intimate relationship with God.

Ministry as Activity

Ministry as activity (applying the function) describes action that facilitates the accomplishment of all five functions within the context of the youth program. Ministry is directed toward helping others by using those God-given gifts—in the form of specific activities that utilize abilities, talents, and resources of students. Such help could involve proclamation of the gospel of Jesus Christ through teaching, preaching, singing, and encouraging. It could also take on a more pragmatic role in the form of feeding, healing, protecting, or serving.

A Kingdom-Focused Church Model and Process

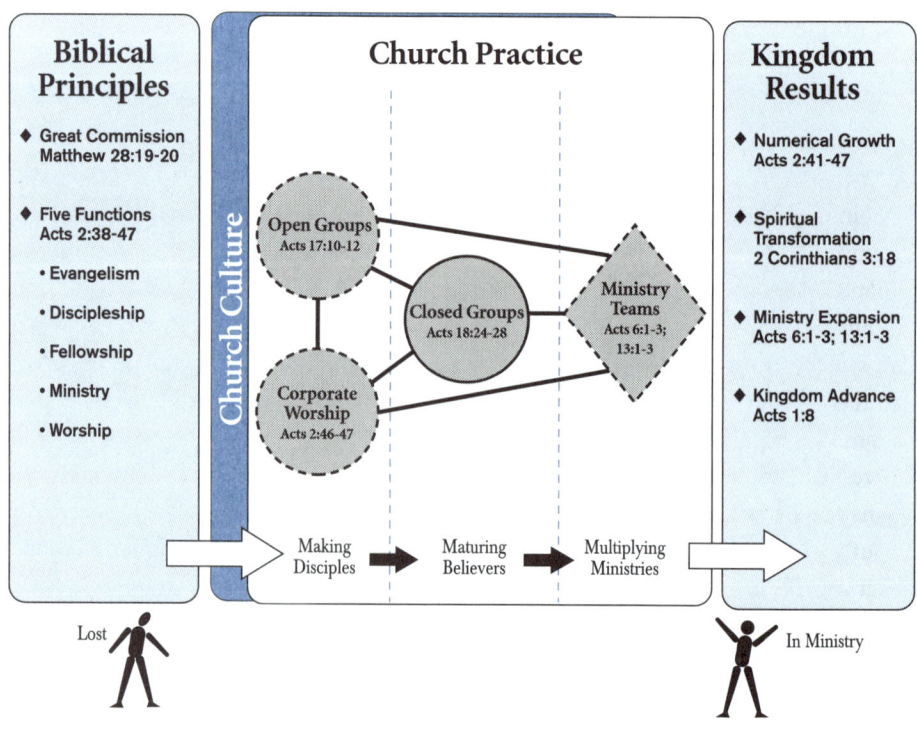

Basic Student Ministry

Ministry in the context of youth programming can be defined as *activities done in the name of Jesus that extend His purposes and mission in the context of the local church.* In addition to regular church programs like Sunday School and discipleship; volunteer projects, service teams, soup kitchens, construction projects—all are very "in" with regard to popularity among teenagers. I believe the cultural changes Melvin Swafford so passionately described in the sidebar (on pp. 67-68) make it all the more critical to *do* ministry as opposed to merely *hearing* about ministry. Facts and stories are great, but transformation happens when application is action. As a Chinese proverb has stated, *What I hear, I forget. What I see, I remember. What I do, I understand.*

Back to the Diagram: Ministry in and Through Ongoing Church Activity

There are five assumptions that precede a discussion of the "doing" of ministry. First, is the personal world of the minister of youth. If there is a person who has been called to (or assigned!) the task of leading the youth ministry, then that person's call, giftedness, family situation, experience, maturity, and even personality necessarily affect the way that ministry is conducted in a particular place. Second, the five functions of youth ministry are assumed to be foundational. In other words, these functions would be constant regardless of the size of the youth group, the geographical location of the church, the presence or absence of a paid youth minister, or any other variable. The personal world and the functions of youth ministry are portable—they travel with the minister of youth if he or she should move to another church.

Third, administration is necessary to facilitate ministry. Richard Ross has done an excellent job describing the process of planning and administration in chapter 6. In one sentence (mine, not Richard's), which sounds like a proverb, "The wise youth minister must manage the business of ministry in order to have continued opportunity and resources to serve." In other words, mission statements and budgets create an environment for ministry to happen. Without effective planning and administration, a youth minister may not have a chance to prove how creative, innovative, and effective he or she is.

Fourth, the process of "targeting" ministry should always have as the goal to move students from spiritual irrelevance ("Crowd"–where a student will take the first steps of becoming a disciple) to a commitment to doing ministry because of Christ ("Group" and "Committed"—a maturing/multiplying disciple) and ultimately to lead others in doing ministry ("Multiplier"). I found this flow in two chapters of Scripture, Luke 9 and 10. (See chapter 2.)[14]

Fifth, the cultural context and the condition of adult/youth relationships in a particular setting provide the "box" within which ministry or programming activities take place. Initially, such programming is expressed via activities (or meetings) involving various types of groups, namely open groups, closed groups, and ministry teams. It is important to remember that the church has a heritage and, at the very least, this heritage should be considered before the youth ministry launches into various approaches to ministry. The youth ministry is in part a ministry team of the overall church and should not be in conflict with the direction of the church and leadership of the pastor. Although, it is possible for the youth ministry to lead the way at times or initiate a new and different slant on ministry. The needs that exist within cultural context of the church can and should be addressed through the ministry of the church.

OPEN GROUPS

Open groups are those characterized by ready access. In context of youth ministry, "open" means both believers and unbelievers are invited to participate in any and all Bible studies, classes, departments, study groups, small groups, cell groups, Wednesday night events, retreats, or any other event that has an intentional evangelistic purpose in a small group Bible study context—every time the group meets.

An open group is an entry point into the youth ministry. It provides a nonthreatening environment for a student who is investigating what it might mean to begin a relationship with Christ. The constant question in the mind of one who leads an open group is *what is the next step?* The movement from Step One: "Come and See" to Step Five: "Ministry Above and Beyond" as Randy Fields suggested, indicates that Randy and his staff have thought about successive steps toward maturity ("up the ladder"). As he said, "each step must be completed before the next step."

In describing the "what's next?" progression, an open group also assimilates students into the youth ministry. At the same time, an open group intentionally focuses on "sending out" members as witnesses and leaders of new groups. In other words, open groups are open on both ends.[15] They are conduits of the gospel enterprise—receiving, assimilating, providing a base for making disciples, and then sending out. In summary, open groups, mean that both believers and nonbelievers are invited to participate every time the group meets. I have heard several youth ministers use the metaphor of the "empty chair" for an open group, asking, "Who should be in this chair the next time we meet?"

Open groups do not require advance preparation on the part of the student. The leader is prepared to answer questions, follow up discussion, and foster continued relationships as an outflow of the open group meeting. Traditionally, Sunday School has been considered to be the primary open group strategy in a youth ministry and still is the best practice of an open group strategy, but in the last decade or two, weeknight youth meetings and/or worship also have become the front door to many youth ministries. Other open groups could be retreats or camps, targeted events at church, or seasonal emphases designed in small group settings that are open to both believers and nonbelievers. The key factors in healthy open groups are the accepting environment and an understanding by the leadership of the role of the open group in the movement of a student from "Crowd" to "Group" to "Committed" to "Multiplier".

Open Groups and Ministry

Framing in the context of ministry being "youth group turned outward," think about a place where every individual student is loved and wanted. The needs of the students within each open group should be taken very seriously and be addressed through ministry by the leaders and fellow class or open group members. In a culture where too many unloved and unwanted teenagers exist, even the environment can minister.

Teenagers today are incredibly busy, but if a session flows so that leaders and learners remain focused on God's Word and on the application to their lives, students will understand the relevance of a relationship with Christ. If teaching methods are varied, and biblical truth is creatively presented, then Sunday's lesson becomes Monday's lifestyle, and the "what next" question is ready to be asked.

In addition to the environment, which can minister to teenagers who come upon an invitation from a friend, open groups can actively minister as a group. A glamourous application of an open group involved in ministry would be a mission trip or leadership in a worship service. On the less visible side of things, a Sunday School class can adopt a family at Christmas, clean up a section of highway, offer tutoring for an elementary school, or volunteer to mow the lawn at the church. If open groups are to be successful and healthy, ministry must be a part of its strategy both to its open group participants and for its participants to partner together and engage in ministry to the community.

CLOSED GROUPS

I believe that in the New Testament, Jesus initiated closed groups. We know that He fed five thousand folks who were interested in physical and spiritual food. We know He had 70 volunteers to go on an evangelistic crusade. When He got ready to pick His disciples, He only chose 12. I have wondered how Jesus decided who was ready for what type of teaching or experience, but it is evident that He did not consider all of His followers to be alike. Some of them were ready for deeper things. Perhaps God had a specialized challenge or maybe they had a unique set of gifts that matched a particular teaching or ministry need. Maybe they were simply ready for a deeper level of commitment. At any rate, there were groups that consisted of increasingly fewer people in more intimate settings.

Paul Turner, discipleship and closed group specialist at LifeWay, described *closed groups* as those that:
- Build kingdom leaders
- Create an environment for equipping
- Equip persons for service
- Multiply
- Exist for a season or for a purpose

Typically, closed groups have referred to discipleship groups. While I was in seminary, I was taught that the content areas for the part of the youth program (then called Discipleship Training) targeted to those who were believers in Christ were:
- Theology (right understanding about God)
- Doctrine (right biblical thinking about church practices)
- Christian ethics (right application regarding moral issues)
- Christian history (legacy of those before us)
- Church polity (the organization of church)

It was generally believed that the "discipleship" arm of youth ministry equipped leaders. Staying in the boundaries of this chapter, it is the preparation stage for ministry. In other words, "Group" and "Committed" students were challenged to dig a little deeper into what it means to mature in Christ, thus equipping them to turn their relationships with Christ outward, thus multiplying their ministries.

In Acts 18, Apollos was preaching when Priscilla and Aquilla approached him to say there was more to the picture than he understood. They explained the way of faith more accurately to him. Discipleship in the New Testament church was born.

> **A Jew named Apollos, a native Alexandrian, an eloquent man who was powerful in the Scriptures, arrived in Ephesus. The man had been instructed in the way of the Lord; and being fervent in spirit, he spoke and taught the things about Jesus accurately, although he knew only John's baptism. He began to speak boldly in the synagogue. After Priscilla and Aquilla heard him, they took him home and explained the way of God to him more accurately (Acts 18:25-26).**

The greatest thing I believe that God is teaching us is about developing a team in student ministry leadership (adults). This is very difficult in today's society and seems to be getting more difficult. We need adults to walk with students. We have heard the statement "I want to teach, but I really don't have the time to walk with students."

With every intern I have had, I have had them go through the activity of developing a six-month student ministry calendar as if they were starting as the student pastor of a new church. Never has one of these interns, often those who feel called into the ministry, included in their calendar the aspect of building a team of youth workers through recruitment, training, fellowship, discipleship, and so on. All these aspiring youth pastors can see is the ministry with the teenagers and their needs, activities, and so on. They do not understand the need to build a team of workers who can help them as student pastors walk with, care for, disciple students, plus, continue the ministry as God may move us to another assignment as you and I know. So, thinking in terms of things that upcoming student pastors need to know or need to be equipped with, we feel this might be a great tool and truth for their ministry.
—Melvin Swafford
FBC, Cleveland, Tennessee

Closed Groups and Ministry

Closed groups are not holy huddles where Christians love on each other. *Closed* means they are closed for specific training for awhile, or to address specific needs of individuals. Churches may have lost the idea that discipleship and maturity take time. The purpose of the discipleship ministry of the church has been to help persons to mature so they could in turn help others. Paul said to Timothy, "And what you have heard from me in the presence of many witnesses, commit to faithful men who will be able to teach others also" (2 Tim. 2:2). The developing of disciples develops leaders (both adult and student) who will assist in guiding the church to effective ministry.

An example of a closed group that becomes a ministry team would be a mission team. Suppose a youth group was going to take a mission trip to a foreign country. They would need a certain level of competence in order to work effectively in an international setting. Language, customs, and ministry skills need to be acquired or sharpened. A closed group would allow a team to train progressively for the trip. If someone were allowed to join the group a week or two before departure, they would not be prepared.

It is also important to remember that ministry is an important element within a closed group. Even if the closed group is closed for the purpose of equipping for ministry, the members within the closed group have needs that can be met by caring and concerned members who are a part of that group. Closed groups might also exist for the sole purpose of ministry to the members. If a team of high school juniors and seniors were equipped to disciple a group of seventh and eighth graders, the closed nature of those relationships fosters the trust needed for growth.

MINISTRY TO AND WITH ADULTS

One point we need to make is that ministry to adults connected to teenagers (adult youth leaders and parents of youth) is an important aspect of youth ministry. If open and closed groups are opportunities for students to gather, be ministered to, and ultimately to minister, why not include adult groups as well? Back in the '70s, Bob Taylor suggested the "one-third, one-third, one-third" principle in which the wise youth minister would realize that a third of his or her time would be spent with youth, a third with parents of youth, and the remaining third with adults who volunteer to work with youth. Radical at the time, the idea shook a common conception of youth ministry that perceived the job description of the youth minister as programming for and hanging out exclusively with teenagers. Taylor advocated the involvement of adults for at least two reasons. First, there is value in having several voices to reinforce the Christian teaching in youth ministry. Second, and probably as vital, was the likelihood that those adults would be influencing teenagers in that youth ministry long after the youth minister had moved on.

Basic Student Ministry

In our current context, if ministry is to be intentional to teenagers and ministering is to be facilitated with teenagers, then the adults who are connected to the youth ministry should be included as well. Often, these adults do not regularly attend an open or closed group of adults, but spend their "church time" with students. If they are not targeted for ministry and for ministering in the same way as teenagers, they could end up being left out all together. Many youth ministers have understood the need for ministry to adult volunteers and have been thanked for:

- Remembering a birthday or anniversary
- Keeping an "open door" for youth workers
- Giving holiday surprises (Valentine cards, Christmas stockings, Easter cards)
- Sending personal notes to recognize accomplishments
- Sending thank you notes—don't take for granted that they did the lock-in because they wanted to…

Adult volunteers are perhaps the key to success in creating student ministry teams (open and closed groups) that are effective. If a person is a paid youth minister, I believe their number one priority is to establish a team of adult volunteers who can assist with all aspects of the ministry.

In addition to ministering with and to adult volunteers, parents are an important part of youth ministry programming. In my classes, I mention "Building Blocks for Ministry with Parents" as a reminder of this vital group:

Counseling
- Counsel with youth, with parents, with families.
- Counsel with warmth, genuineness (knowledgeable, but not Messiah), and empathy.
- Counsel with a view on referral. A wise youth minister gets training in family issues so he or she can know when to refer to a professional counselor.

Calendaring
- Calendar for parents. (Consider things like parent's night out, parent Bible study, Sunday School department for parents of teenagers, seminars, and support groups.)
- Calendar with parents in mind. (Don't schedule the end of the lock-in at 6:00 a.m. on a Saturday morning.)
- Calendar with caution. (You don't have to schedule a youth meeting during exam week and families love you if you leave some holidays unscheduled.)

Communicating
- Communicate through parent networking meetings or seminars.
- Communicate through newsletters and publicity (concerning youth activities as well as parent events).

Connecting
- Connect with competent and trusted referral agents.
- Connect with community events.
- Connect with good books or other resources.

Adult Groups as Ministry Teams

In each of the chapters of this book, you will read of the involvement of adults in ministry teams. In addition to lead teams (ministry teams responsible for planning and implementing specific events—discussed in chapter 6), outreach teams, open and closed group leadership, and so forth, think of ways adults can minister with their families. The family mission trip can be one of the most important times family members can share. Perhaps you can consider a special trip just for families. For students who attend without a family, assign them to another family to be an "honorary family member" for the duration of the trip. Families eat together, work together, and play together.

Feet to the Faith: Ministry Teams

When open, closed, or adult groups are turned outward for missions and inward for service, creativity has been demonstrated by many youth ministers in meeting the needs of others. Though some of these have already been suggested, the summary is helpful. Some examples I have discovered among youth ministries include:

- *Mission trips.*—A group of students is equipped to serve in a specific location to assist existing ministries or to establish new ones. Many youth groups go on mission trips to partner with domestic or foreign missionaries who are already in place.
- *Family mission trips.*—Merton Strommen has said for years that a mission experience alongside parents is the strongest discipleship that a student can have.
- *Parent ministry.*—Ministering to the needs of parents. Counseling tips for youth ministers to help parents.
- *Peer ministry.*—Via tutoring or discipleship, students are trained to help other students with anything from mathematics homework to learning how to share their faith.
- *After school tutoring.*—Not limited to peers, some students are volunteering to assist children who are struggling with academics. Especially appreciated by single moms.
- *Puppet teams.*—The good news is shared via creative ministry with puppets.
- *Drama teams.*—The good news is shared via dramatic arts.
- *Clowning teams.*—Students and adults are equipped to minister and share the gospel through clowning.
- *Sign language teams.*—In a visual culture, the message can be signed as well as spoken.
- *Acteens® Activators.*—The teenaged girls' mission arm of the Women's Missionary Union is still having incredible effectiveness sending prepared young women into mission experiences.
- *World Changers, work camps, M-Fuge.*—Mission trips with a specific focus to fix, repair, rebuild, or construct.
- *Lead teams.*—Small groups of students and adults who take ownership for ministry events. Not a work team, but ultimately responsible for the event.
- *Youth council.*—A group of students who serve as advisors to the youth ministry leader for the planning and direction of the student ministry.

- *SWAT (students with a testimony).*—This innovative ministry trains high school students to serve as Bible study leaders for DiscipleNow weekends.
- *Black light teams.*—A creative youth minister in Louisiana coached a group of teenagers to perform routines in black light staging. The students wear all-black outfits with fluorescent scarves and gloves. The students disappear into the blackness, with only the accessories visible.
- *Youth praise band, choirs, ensembles, orchestras.*—Students with talent or willingness in artistic areas lead in worship for youth and churchwide services.
- *Card ministry.*—One youth worker told of an unusually good perception of the youth ministry by the adults due to the "card ministry." The youth in the church had begun to write cards of encouragement to senior adults that opened lines of communication and initiated some positive intergenerational relationships.
- *Mission Lab New Orleans.*—A response by the New Orleans Baptist Theological Seminary to utilize dormitory space for mission groups during the summer. Mission Lab has expanded to include senior adults and college students.

What is the bottom line? Students want to be active in ministry. Students who are believers inevitably grow in Christian maturity as a result of such experiences. A ministry team, however, may have another purpose—evangelism. Sometimes ministry teams can be used as a part of an evangelistic process. If lost teenagers are allowed to be part of ministry teams, it is possible they may be drawn to the authenticity of a relationship with Christ.

Ministry That Leads to Faith

One discussion that has been conducted in youth ministry circles is that which ponders what kind of worship, discipleship, or ministry a non-Christian can do. We debate whether or not a nonbeliever can worship and the consensus seems to be that only one who knows God can truly worship Him, although non-Christians can be drawn to the awesomeness of God as they watch Christians worship (which is why we sing praise music at a "seeker" service).

We wonder if a non-Christian can be discipled, and Erwin McManus rightly points out that pre-evangelism, awareness of God, and even conversion are all aspects of discipleship.

> *Discipleship happens before evangelism—mostly we think that it is the other way around. Jesus said, "Go and make disciples" and we think that is about Christians. When Jesus said that, there were only a few disciples. They weren't called to disciple each other—they were called to make disciples of all nations. At the time, all nations were pagan. Peter was told to "feed my sheep." The paradigm that would have come to mind was that the shepherd left the ninety-nine to go after the one.*
>
> *The question that we have to be ready to answer is the one that is posed by everyone ultimately in a pantheistic universalistic culture: "Why should I accept Jesus as the only way—what about the people in India…?" Are we so egocentric that we believe that God who can move mountains is not already at work in India? The reason that people can make a decision for Christ is that they have been discipled first. We [at Mosaic, McManus' Los Angeles church] don't use the language of "receiving Christ" because that would imply that we are stationary.*[16]

We also anguish as youth ministers about whether to take non-Christian teenagers on a mission trip, let them play guitar in the youth praise band, or volunteer for a leadership position in the youth group. Does the spiritual immaturity or lack of Bible knowledge prohibit ministry from happening? Should service in the name of Christ and His church be accomplished exclusively by believers? Ministry teams can be extremely effective entry points into a church's youth group.

Tony Campolo, in his book, *The Church and the American Teenager,* suggests a result of ministry he calls *praxis*.[17] Stay with me here. Borrowing a term from the counseling profession, he proposes that in many cases, a young person intuitively feels what the truth is, but has not made a profession of faith in Jesus. If a student is allowed and even encouraged to participate in ministry, Campolo asserts that, "what a person does determines what a person thinks. In short, action determines ideology; action determines what one believes to be real; action determines religious convictions… If a Christian is someone who believes in Jesus, then according to the praxis principle, doing the things Jesus would do makes a person a believer."[18] While this may sound controversial, it helps me to understand why many teenagers "get it" concerning the validity of their faith when they do a mission project.

Learning takes place in all three learning domains: cognitive (thinking), affective (feeling), and behavioral (doing). Open and closed groups that are designed to teach facts deal with the cognitive (knowledge and understanding)—knowledge of the truth is grasped, remembered, and processed. Stories, role plays, media, and even mission projects led by the youth minister or other adults move into the affective domain (attitudes and convictions); convictions, feelings, attitudes, or emotions are developed regarding the truth encountered.

When students are given an outlet for the knowledge and attitudes that have been gained or facilitated, the behavioral domain (lifestyle and skills) is entered. Changes are consciously made in behavior based upon the processing of the truth. In turn, the knowledge gained in open and closed groups is revisited, the attitudes formed in the application of cognitive information are reinforced, and the ministry actions are more likely to be ongoing. In other words (as Campolo said), teenagers who act out their faith are in fact developing their faith.

Ministry Evaluation

So how do we know if all of this ministry is "working"? Evaluation in ministry is a touchy subject for many youth ministers. Often, we are called upon to give an account of how we spend our time and the church's money. The part of the MAP diagram called "results" may be more resonant in terms of "success." We are not guaranteed results, but we can measure the effectiveness of our ministry.

Basic Student Ministry

We cannot evaluate ministry success unless we know needs and set goals. (See chapter 6.) Good assessment is primary to ministry design. In discovering needs that can be addressed through youth ministry and ministry action, we use:
- Tools to discover ministry needs
- Tools to discover ministry giftedness (spiritual gifts—how to put them into perspective and do things out of students' giftedness)
- Tools to discover needs in the community around our church

Once we have articulated a mission statement, developed a strategy to move students through commitment levels from "Crowd" to "Multiplier", helped them mature in their faith, and designed processes to implement that strategy, we can also use evaluative tools to measure the effectiveness of our efforts. Usually, our effectiveness has been measured in terms of numbers. But numbers of what? baptisms? additional group members? amount of teenagers who went to summer camp? I believe these designations are too ambiguous to provide effective feedback.

I suggest the four "results" categories from the MAP diagram (p. 70) allow us to evaluate our ministry actions. The measures of success are:
- Numerical.—How many teenagers are involved in this ministry?
- Spiritual.—How many teenagers are growing spiritually because of this ministry?
- Ministry.—How many new ministries have been created to address various needs that have been identified?
- Kingdom.—How is the greater community being affected by this ministry?

You might accuse me of merely repackaging the numbers game. Yes, numbers are perhaps the only quantitative measure of growth or effectiveness. I hope you are encouraged, however, by the notion that you count students who are involved in a number of types of ministry action, and not just attendance.

Another evaluative measure is that of standards. We ask for commitment from leaders and students but we are told it is not kosher for the church to place such "demands." Yet, coaches, band directors, dance instructors, and so on are placing more and more demands on students, families, and their time and that is seen not only as OK, but as needed—by our society and our church. So when we need to establish a regular workers' meeting or ask students to commit to a discipleship process— "well, we just don't have the time" or "that is asking too much." When we see students adopting godly standards, wisely choosing friends, breaking habits, adopting godly lifestyles—which may require considerable sacrifice or commitment—then we know (spiritual growth) our ministry has been effective and that God is honored.

Conclusion

Ten thousand students stood in seven cities on the last day of 1999 during YouthLink 2000 and indicated they were willing to be used by God in proclaiming the gospel and in doing missions work at home and around the world. I was in Houston, in the Astro Hall, and I watched teenagers volunteering for significant ministry. I was impressed with a sense of responsibility—it is my generation who has to help this intent to become reality. Richard Ross has been the leading voice in asking the question, "what if this group of 'third millennium teens' is the generation of students whom God has prepared to witness His return?" Mark Matlock in his book, *Generation Hope* said it this way:

Through years of nationwide ministry to teenagers, I have studied the trends of the youth culture and how the gospel can shape today's student generation to fulfill God's will. As I studied and prayed, God gave me a fresh perspective—a powerful, compelling perspective—about this generation of young men and women. They are in a unique position to have a historic impact on the world. The resources of funding, communication, and travel give them the opportunity to fulfill the Great Commission, to take the gospel of Christ to every group of people throughout the entire planet![19]

Findley Edge said a church exists by ministry [mission] as a fire exists by burning. Ministry is both the intent and the result of taking the claims of Christ seriously. The model of youth ministry that is being suggested is one that considers ministry as both a function and an action. The action is an extension of the function and is carried out by the various gatherings of persons, both youth and adult, who participate in a ministry to youth in a local setting.

My favorite quote is that of Admiral Yamamoto of the Japanese Imperial Navy, as he assessed the results of the bombing of Pearl Harbor on December 7, 1941, and the impact on the American people. He said, "We had hoped to deliver a crippling and demoralizing blow, but what I fear is that we have awakened a sleeping giant and filled him with a terrible resolve." My prayer is the sleeping giant of an 80 million-person generation is awakened to the opportunities to serve Jesus by being involved in ministry action.

---

[1] Mark Senter, "Axioms of Youth Ministry," in *The Complete Book of Youth Ministry* (Chicago: Moody Press, 1999).
[2] Warren Benson, "A Theology of Youth Ministry" in *The Complete Book of Youth Ministry* (Chicago: Moody Press, 1987), 20.
[3] Randy Fields, "Developing a Youth Ministry Philosophy," online article at *www.lifeway.com*, accessed 12/11/02.
[4] Merton Strommen, "A Recent Invention: The Profession of Youth Ministry," in Karen Jones and Dave Rahn, *Youth Ministry that Transforms* (Grand Rapids: Zondervan/Youth Specialties, 2001), 27.
[5] Mark Senter and Richard Dunn, *Reaching a Generation for Christ* (Chicago: Moody Press, 1997), 106-107.
[6] Ross, Richard, ed. *The Work of the Minister of Youth* (Nashville: Convention Press, 1989), 11.
[7] Doug Fields, *Purpose Driven Youth Ministry* (Grand Rapids: Zondervan Publishing Co., 1998), 46. Also see Gene Mims, *Kingdom Principles for Church Growth, Revised and Expanded* (Nashville: LifeWay Press, 2001).
[8] Gene Mims, *Kingdom Principles for Church Growth, Revised and Expanded* (Nashville: LifeWay Press, 2001), 50.
[9] Frank Stagg, *New Testament Theology* (Nashville: Broadman Press, 1962), 250.
[10] Ibid, 251.
[11] Mims, 54.
[12] John Stott, *Involvement: Being a Responsible Christian in a Non-Christian Society* (Old Tappan: Fleming H. Revell Company, 1985), 23.
[13] Ibid, 30.
[14] In *Purpose Driven Youth Ministry,* Doug Fields has suggested five target audiences: community, crowd, congregation, committed, and core. For this discussion, the distinctions are collapsed into crowd, group, committed, and multiplier. The multiplier, unlike the other distinctions, may need specialized attention regardless of their spiritual maturity.
[15] Allen Jackson and Richard Barnes, *Teaching Youth: Leaders, Lessons, and Lifestyles* (Nashville: Lifeway Press, 2001).
[16] Erwin McManus in a presentation to the Association of Youth Ministry Educators, 28 October 2002, San Diego, CA. This quote is a transcription from my personal notes.
[17] Tony Campolo, *The Church and the American Teenager* (Grand Rapids: Zondervan/Youth Specialties, 1989), 112.
[18] Ibid.
[19] Mark Matlock, *Generation Hope* (Friendswood: Baxter Press/Wisdom Works Ministries, 2002)

chapter 5
WORSHIP

Scott Stevens

True worship should lead worshipers to a deeper appreciation for God, a better understanding of His ways, and to a deeper commitment to Him. Encountering God in worship transforms us more and more into His likeness.
—Gene Mims, Vice President LifeWay Church Resources

"WORSHIP IS THE EVER-PRESENT, never-ceasing, simple song a Christian always sings. At times the song is fast and loud, then soft and slow, and at times barely above a whisper, barely moving at all. The Christian's song is one that is not always heard, but seen…so I suppose you could call it a miracle. Christians are their own one-man bands. Their hearts sing lead, while their faces sing back up; their feet keep the beat, and their hands respond to the rhythm—rhythm brought about by listening ears waiting for just the right pitch from their Heavenly Leader.

"I have heard many pitches in my four years of being a Christian, and I have danced in the rains of both sorrow and refreshment, and have crawled through deserts of despair. In all I have simply lived…ever singing. And because I have lived for my Lord, I have worshiped; and because I have worshiped, I have a life worth singing about. Worship is not just my song; worship is my lifestyle. Worship is what I was made to do and do well."
—Amanda, 17, San Antonio, Texas

Therefore, brothers, by the mercies of God, I urge you to present your bodies as a living sacrifice, holy and pleasing to God; this is our spiritual worship. Do not be conformed to this age, but be transformed by the renewing of your mind, so that you may discern what is the good, pleasing, and perfect will of God (Rom. 12:1-2).

Wow! Is that a great description of worship or what? Are the words and sentiment expressed by Amanda similar to those used by your students when they describe worship? There is no doubt there has been an explosion of interest and participation in worship among students over the past several years. It has been exciting to witness this seismic shift in focus as teenagers and college students, hungry to encounter the living God, have gathered in a variety of settings to experience worship. Could this be yet another sign God is up to something special among this generation?

When feelings become the purpose and goal of worship, emotional stimuli and external aids will be used to reach that goal. The result is the same kind of manipulation used in television, movies, music, and video games.
—LaMar Boschman, *Future Worship*, Ventura: Renew Books, 1999, 54.

As student ministry leaders, we have the awesome privilege and responsibility not only to educate our students about Christian worship and lead them in worship experiences, but also to model the lifestyle of an authentic worshiper before them. In addition, we can provide worship resources for our teenagers and seek to create opportunities for them to exercise their gifts and talents in leading worship. We must take a holistic view of what it means to worship God as we seek to "Love the LORD (our) God with all (our) heart and with all (our) soul and with all (our) strength" (Deut. 6:5).

So, just how does this happen? What can we do for our students that will help them have intimate encounters with God in both private and public settings? How do we encourage them to broaden their concept of worship? Can we help them recognize that authentic worship may begin as a "service" in the sanctuary on Sunday morning, but should expand to a lifestyle of service and sacrifice? These are some weighty questions. Let's begin to consider the answers by laying some groundwork on the subject of worship.

Some Thoughts About Worship

It is with a good deal of fear and trepidation that I attempt to cover the subject of worship. This topic is both deep and wide, and encompasses intimate experiences with the Creator of the universe! In fact, when I think about those times when I have had a particularly close encounter with the Father, words are inadequate to convey the depth and meaning of the experience. That being said, let's explore this incredible, indescribable experience together.

Human beings are great worshipers. If you don't believe me, just go to any number of sporting events in and around your community. Not only will people be yelling and screaming encouragement to their favorite players and teams, they will be decked out in the colors, logos, and mascots of these teams. Think about those folks who follow NASCAR®. These folks show up days before the big race in their RVs, hoping to get a glimpse of their favorite driver, all the while wearing a T-shirt with said driver's face and car number emblazoned on it.

It doesn't stop with sports. What about the worship and adoration afforded movie stars, television personalities, and recording artists? We often spare no expense in terms of the time, money, attention, and affection we lavish on the rich and famous. Why is that?

The fact is man was *created for worship* and *we will worship* God or find someone or something else to worship. Louie Giglio, leader of Passion Ministries, has stated that worship is what we do all day long every day. He says the ongoing activity of the human soul is to seek something of value and worship it. In this sense, our true worship is determined by how we live, not just by what we sing or say at church. Louie also says the problem often

Basic Student Ministry

is not that we are inadequate as worshipers, but that we have chosen an inadequate object of worship—someone or something unworthy of our affection and devotion.[1]

The word *worship* has its roots in the words *worth-ship,* which mean *one worthy of reverence and honor.* When we worship God, we are declaring His worthiness as the only One deserving of our total love and devotion. Here are a few other thoughts about worship:

- **Worship is not a human invention; it is a divine offer.** This is not something we were bright enough to think of, but something for which we were created to enjoy as the crown of God's creation: a chance to relate to Him through worship.
- **Worship is an end in itself; it is not a means to something else.** If we engage in worship for the sake of certain benefits we hope to receive, the act ceases to be worship. We may start to treat God as a "good luck charm" who "owes" us something because of the attention we have given Him. That is not worship.
- **Worship is not mere preparation for action.** Although we may be inspired to action because of an encounter with God in worship, we worship God simply because He is worthy of our reverence and honor.[2]

What thoughts come to your mind when you think about worship? There are probably as many definitions of worship as there are worshipers. Instead of trying to land on a definition at this time, consider the following descriptions of worship and see if they resonate with your experience. Worship can be described as:

Mystery—Worship is mystery in that God both reveals and withholds Himself at the same time. He is both *immanent* (close enough for us to relate to) and *transcendent* (beyond our comprehension). We should approach worship with a sense of mystery, awe, and wonder. The truth is, we don't have this down! In fact, I don't want to worship a God I have completely figured out (like that would be possible!).

Celebration—Worship is a celebration of God's acts in history (creation, redemption, covenants, Jesus, the Holy Spirit, etc.) and of His acts in our lives (salvation, family, relationships, His presence, spiritual victories, comfort). We have much to celebrate, and worship can provide a meaningful outlet as we rejoice in the Lord.

Life—Worship is not limited to what we do in "big church." It is related to every area of our lives. The way we treat others, the effort we give at our jobs or in our studies, and the attitudes we exhibit are all part of our worship. These things are telling and showing others the value we ascribe to God and to our relationship with Jesus Christ.

Dialogue—Worship is both revelation and response. God takes the initiative in revelation and man responds in worship and is transformed. Worship is more than conversation, it is an encounter (think of Isaiah as recorded in Isaiah 6). One of the amazing things about this dialogue is that meaningful worship leads to decisive experiences and change. Whether or not we walk an aisle, when we have an authentic encounter with God, we are left with the decision of how we will respond to the encounter. If there is no transformation, there is no worship.

Giving—Worship is not just about getting blessed by God. It also involves blessing God and others by the giving of our money, our time, and our possessions to further His purposes in the world. Other types of giving could include committing to live in sincere faith and total obedience to the Lord. When was the last time you entered a worship service thinking about what you could give to bless God?[3]

Hopefully these descriptions are helpful. While it seems Christian worship tends to defy definition, perhaps its essence can be best described as inner experiences that lead to outward acts. This is key for living a lifestyle of worship.

> *By pursuing the trivial and worshiping things that offer a temporary feeling of self-importance and security, we have all sentenced ourselves to a futile and fruitless struggle for that original Garden fulfillment. But as Adam would tell you, it's a pointless, dead-end journey until we rediscover our identity as worshipers of the only true God.*
> —Mercy Me with Jeff Kinley, *I Can Only Imagine,* Nashville: Nelson Bibles 2002, 21.

Ascribe to the LORD the glory due His name: bring an offering and come before Him. Worship the LORD in His holy majesty (1 Chron. 16:29).

Attitudes that Express Worship

It has been stated that attitude is everything. Maybe this is because our attitudes reveal the condition of our hearts—not the blood-pumping muscle in our chests, but that confluence of our minds, emotions, and wills. The inner experiences of true worship often involve significant changes in the attitudes of the worshiper. Some attitudes that express worship include:

1. **Adoration, expressed in praise.**—Have you ever noticed that when you adore someone, you feel compelled to offer him or her praise? This praise is not fake nor does it have to be manufactured. It just seems to flow out of our mouths. It is the same in worship. When we recognize God for who He truly is, we can't help but praise Him.
2. **Gratitude, expressed in thanksgiving.**—Have you made a list lately of all you have to be thankful for? I know my tendency is to take God's blessings for granted. This kind of attitude should be replaced with a recognition of the scope and magnitude of the blessings God has allowed me to enjoy. Such recognition must be followed by concrete expressions of thanksgiving to God and to people He has used to bless my life.
3. **Repentance, expressed through humility and confession.**—We must agree with God about our sin and then commit, in His power and strength, to turn from our sin and follow the Savior. Confession is the starting point, not the end. Frequently students come to a point of confession in worship, and once the weight of their guilt is lifted, they fail to follow through in true repentance. It is important to help them experience the new beginnings grace affords.
4. **Dependence, asking God for what we need.**—It took me 24 years to realize I am not smart enough or strong enough to make it on my own. Perhaps I'm a slow learner, but I'm guessing I may not be alone in this. Our God is the only One who is powerful enough to meet all our needs. Worship is a time when we can express our total dependence on Him.
5. **Submission, surrendering to God's will.**—Often the greatest struggle in living the Christian life is not in discovering God's will, but in surrendering to what we know plainly to be the will of God. Things such as sharing Christ with others, growing in spiritual maturity, and loving others require us to submit our human, selfish desires to the lordship of Christ. Such submission leads to a lifestyle of worship.
6. **Commitment, willingly dedicating ourselves to God.**—It seems as though the concept of commitment has become a short-term reality in our world. Commitments only last until someone gets tired or bored. Encountering God in worship will lead us to respond in commitment to Him and His purposes for our lives. We can willingly choose to dedicate all we have and all we are to the accomplishment of Christ's reign in our thoughts and actions.[4]

Now here's the hard part. How about an attitude check? As you look over these six descriptions, how accurately do they express your attitudes in worship and your attitudes about worship? As you may know, students tend to pick up their leaders' attitudes about many things, worship included. Let's be honest, when it comes to worship are our attitudes worth emulating?

The heart of worship is surrender.
—Rick Warren, *The Purpose-Driven Life,* Grand Rapids: Zondervan, 2002, 77.

The Priority of Prayer in Worship

Jesus once said, "It is written, 'My house will be a house of prayer,' but you have made it a 'den of thieves'" (Luke 19:46). He uttered these words as He cleansed the temple area of unscrupulous salesmen. When it comes to the worship at your church and in your student ministry, is God's house a house of prayer? Not to stretch this metaphor too far, but could it be that one of the reasons many churches seem impotent in impacting our communities for Christ is because we have placed doing things for God (programs, etc.) above pouring out our hearts to God? In doing so, have we robbed ourselves of both His direction and His power?

Ron Owens, in his book *Return to Worship: A God-centered Approach,* offers some piercing commentary on this topic. Contemplate the following statement: "It seems the more we excel in man's mechanics (programs), the less we know of God's dynamics." In some of the churches he has visited, he mentions that more time was spent in welcoming visitors and making the announcements, than was spent in prayer. "There are Christians today who seem to be more interested in getting prayer back in our schools than back in our churches." He also offers these two questions to consider concerning prayer:

1. "Is my personal prayer life commensurate (equal to) the assignment I feel God has given me to be light and salt in the world?"
2. "Is the prayer life of my church commensurate with the assignment and vision God has given us to reach our community and beyond with the gospel?"[5]

Prayer should be a vital part of both our corporate and our personal worship. Silent prayer, pastoral prayers, spontaneous congregational prayer, invocations, benedictions, prayers for offerings, praying in small groups, and reading prayers from the Bible can all be ways to engage the people of God in worthwhile experiences of prayer.

Students and Prayer.—It has been encouraging to see the desire of students in recent years to be involved in times of corporate prayer. The annual See You at the Pole event continues to grow, which is wonderful; but it has also been in student-focused worship meetings where teens really pour out their hearts in prayer.

These students are willing to offer sentence prayers and desperately desire times of intercessory prayer as they share requests that touch on a variety of areas from family and friends to school and personal needs. It has been touching to see them gather around group members who have experienced difficult circumstances and lift them up in prayer and know they are turning to God in intense personal times of intercessory prayer away from religious settings. The strength of integrating a community of students into a student ministry family through prayer cannot be underestimated. Student ministry leaders must not fail to provide their teens these chances to unite with one another and with God in prayer.

The Object of Our Worship

Though it has been stated many times, it deserves repeating: "The audience in our worship is God and God alone."

God is the only One who deserves our praise and adoration and what we offer in worship we offer to Him. This often runs counter to our consumer-driven society's idea of what church should be like. Too often our expectations and evaluations of worship are

As a deer longs for streams of water, so I long for you, God. I thirst for God, the living God. When can I come and appear before God? (Ps. 42:1-2).

Its purpose (worship's) is not to gain numbers nor for our churches to be seen as successful. Rather, the entire reason for our worship is that God deserves it. Moreover, it isn't even useful for earning points with God, for what we do in worship won't change one whit how God feels about us. We will always still be helpless sinners caught in our endless inability to be what we should be or to make ourselves better — and God will always still be merciful, compassionate, and gracious, abounding in steadfast love and ready to forgive us as we come to Him.
—Marva J. Dawn, *A Royal "Waste" of Time: The Splendor of Worshiping God and Being Church for the World,* Grand Rapids: William B. Eerdmans Publishing Company, 1999, 1.

dependent on the talent and skill of the worship leaders. If we didn't like the style of music or if the pastor couldn't make us laugh and keep our undivided attention, we may conclude we have had a poor worship experience. To paraphrase a popular chorus, "It's not all about me!"

Yes, we should give our very best in worship. Musicians should rehearse and preachers should study and pray, and we should prepare our hearts for worship, but we are not the audience—God is. Sometimes this is confusing for people, especially teenagers. We tend to equate people on a platform with being on stage and so those in front of us must be there for our entertainment, right? In some churches, the place of worship has been created to enhance just such an environment with the latest in sound, light, and technology. None of this is bad in and of itself, but sometimes it can be challenging to keep our focus on the One we were created to worship (Rev. 4:11).

Worship Wars?

One of the unfortunate things that has happened in the church in the midst of this swelling emphasis on worship has been the so-called "worships wars." Often the battles are centered on the style of music used in a worship service. What will it be: traditional, contemporary, or blended? Perhaps it's not surprising student ministers have been in the middle of some of these battles as they have advocated a musical style appealing to teenagers.

This is not the first time there have been disagreements over the use of music in worship. The introduction to *The Baptist Hymnal, 1991,* states that in 1690 the Baptist churches in England were involved in a major dispute over whether congregational singing should even be allowed in worship services! Benjamin Keach, a London pastor who believed this opposition to congregational singing was limiting the growth of Baptist churches, published a hymnal in 1691 that included almost three hundred hymns.[6] His efforts have had a far-reaching impact on worship in Baptist churches.

Often the fear of change fuels the fires of these worship wars. While God is the same yesterday, today, and tomorrow, His mercies are also new every day. In the same way, our response to Him in worship should include a balance between these perspectives. Matt Redman has encouraged those responsible for leading worship to remember that, "The key is to somehow find the right balance between the prophetic (the desire to break new ground) and the pastoral (the desire to take people with us). We need to ask the Holy Spirit to give us the insights and wisdom to do this."[7]

George Barna has recently completed a research project on this topic, and his findings suggest that the major issue involved is not the use of music or style of music. Instead, he found that church members have little understanding of what true worship is and how to engage God truly in worship. He has said,

> *Most of the church people who fight about their musical preference do so because they don't understand the relationship between music, communication, God, and worship. Church leaders foster the problem by focus-*

ing on how to please people with music or how to offer enough styles of music to meet everyone's tastes rather than dealing with the underlying issues of limited interest in, comprehension of, and investment in fervent worship of a holy, deserving God.[8]

He also believes that music's place in worship has been overemphasized. Another interesting finding dealt with the difference between church members and church leaders in their perceptions about the purpose of worship. Pastors described the purpose of worship to be "connecting with God" (41%) or "experiencing His presence" (30%), while church members' most prevalent response was that worship was something done for their personal benefit (47%). These findings would seem to indicate a pressing need to educate students, and the church, about the true nature and purpose of worship.[9]

Walt Harrah offers an interesting perspective on the choice of musical style employed in worship saying, "When traditional churches get revived, they start to sing praise songs. When contemporary churches get revived, they'll start to sing church hymns."[10] Perhaps there needs to be more focus on seeking a powerful moving of God's Spirit in the hearts and lives of His people than on the manner in which He will be worshiped. As this happens, the methods in which we choose to praise God will pale in comparison to the awe and utter joy we will experience from drawing close to the Father. The Bible says God is looking for those who will worship Him in spirit and in truth (John 4:23-24). Youth leaders should commit themselves to becoming such worshipers and to helping their students grow in their understanding of authentic worship.

Elmer Towns speaks to the conflict over the style and methodology used in worship by offering, "Worship is like a car to get us from where we are to where God wants us to be. Transportation and communication are imperative; the mode or vehicle is not imperative."[11] He also reminds us that the first murder grew out of a fight over worship (Cain vs. Abel: vegetable vs. blood sacrifice). While today's disagreements over worship are not as violent, they can cause needless division and leave scars on the leaders and congregations affected.

Towns suggests we consider the following questions when encountering controversy over worship methodology:

1. Is this a question of how we worship or Whom we worship?
2. Is this a question of preference or principle?
3. Is this a question of cultural expression or Christian essence?[12]

There are no easy answers here, but whatever the outcome of these conflicts, they should be handled with love, compassion, and understanding. No matter the circumstance in our church, everyone needs to remember that when it comes to worship: *More important than the method of our worship is the object of our worship.*

We worship an audience of One; and He not only deserves our praise and adoration, He desires this time with us even more than the things we attempt for Him.

Why Students Want and Need to Worship

As mentioned, everyone is wired for worship. We are predisposed to seek after something or someone to worship. Students have this built-in desire as well; and in addition, they face changes and challenges from friends, family, the culture, and even their own bodies that heighten their longing

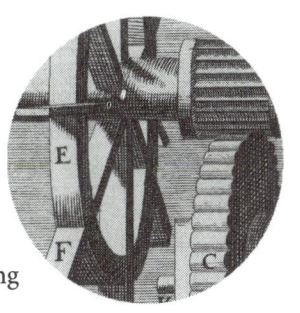

The form of worship is not as important as the purpose of worship. How we worship are expressions of how we feel and how we express those feelings to God. That we worship is far more important than how we worship.
—Gene Mims, Vice President, LifeWay Church Resources.

Making worship more exciting does not always make it more meaningful. True worship can be a powerful, wonderful experience, but it was never intended to be a circus.
—David Hart, "How Should We Use Music in Youth Ministry?", in *Reaching a Generation for Christ*, Richard R. Dunn and Mark H. Senter III. eds, Chicago: Moody Press, 1997, 474.

But an hour is coming, and is now here, when the true worshipers will worship the Father in spirit and truth. Yes, the Father wants such people to worship Him. God is Spirit, and those who worship Him must worship in spirit and truth (John 4:23-24).

Youth and Worship

While still well-represented in the church today, there is a recognizable cultural shift taking place. It is a movement away from the twentieth century emphasis on reason and science, where the Christian faith was explained, proclaimed, and defended, to a faith and theology that is more narrative and less propositional. Because Scripture often utilizes the metaphor of family to describe the community of faith, the worship leaders of our church are committed to the development of a multi-generational worship experience. Ours is not a concern over the elements of worship—hymns versus choruses, hymnals versus projection screens, organ versus keyboard, suits versus blue jeans—but, rather, the content of our worship.

For a generation enamored with the emotional and the experiential, the challenge for pastors and worship leaders in the twenty-first century is the design of a worship experience that "connects" but is, at the same time, substantive. In a narcissistic culture, consumed with self-gratification and self-indulgence, I am fearful that the church has been all too willing to give it what it wants. Many church leaders have been forced by popular, secular thought to sacrifice a biblical theology of worship for one that is seeker-sensitive. The trend of the day seems to be orchestrated toward the worshiper—my preferences, my

to engage in meaningful worship experiences. We know students have physical, mental, emotional, social, and spiritual needs. Authentic Christian worship can play a significant role in meeting these needs. Students want and need to worship because:

1. Their sense of being limited seeks something that is unlimited.

O LORD, our Lord, how magnificent is Your name throughout the earth! You have covered the heavens with Your majesty. Because of Your adversaries, You have established a stronghold from the mouths of children and nursing infants, to silence the enemy and the avenger. When I observe Your heavens, the work of Your fingers, the moon and the stars, which You set in place, what is man that You remember him, the son of man that You look after him? You made him little less than God and crowned him with glory and honor (Ps. 8:1-5).

Students are seeking something or someone bigger than themselves. Many have already realized that their strength and power (and even the strength and power of their parents, schools, and government institutions) is ultimately limited. They desire connection to the all-knowing, ever-present, all-powerful God of the universe and can make this connection in worship.

2. Their sense of insecurity seeks refuge.

God is our refuge and strength, a helper who is always found in times of trouble. Therefore we will not be afraid, though the earth trembles and the mountains topple into the depths of the seas, though its waters roar and foam and the mountains quake with its turmoil (Ps. 46:1-3).

Teenagers are also in search of stability in their lives. The fear and apprehension they feel as they consider their futures in a post 9-11 world is understandable. In addition, many have experienced the disintegration of their families through divorce or other trauma, while others have been uprooted from their environments because of uncertain economic conditions and the job changes that inevitably follow. In the midst of these circumstances, teenagers crave the sense of security found and nurtured in a relationship with Jesus Christ as it is celebrated in worship.

3. Their need to belong to a group seeks fellowship with others.

For as the body is one and has many parts, and all the parts of that body, though many, are one body—so also is Christ. For we were all baptized by one Spirit into one body—whether Jews or Greeks, whether slaves or free—and we were all made to drink of one Spirit (1 Cor. 12:12-13)

Most students are very interested in belonging to a group. As the body of Christ joins together for worship, teens can experience a unique kind of fellowship that is spiritual in nature. It's almost as if the Holy Spirit dwelling inside of each believer facilitates both a broadening and deepening of human relationships. Our students desire relationships with their peers and can benefit from meaningful relationships with adults as well. Times of worship should afford students an opportunity to develop these relationships in an atmosphere of love and acceptance in corporate worship experiences that are both youth oriented and intergenerational (churchwide).

4. Their sense of guilt seeks forgiveness and restoration.

Be gracious to me, God, according to Your faithful love; according to Your abundant compassion, blot out my rebellion. Wash away my guilt, and cleanse me from my sin. For I am conscious of my rebellion, and my sin is always before me. Against You—You alone—I have sinned and done evil in Your sight. So You are right when You pass sentence . . . God, create a clean heart for me and renew a steadfast spirit within me (Ps. 51:1-4,10).

One thing that is bound to happen when we meet God in worship is the overwhelming realization of our sinfulness. It has been stated that our souls are laid bare in worship. When this happens, feelings of guilt can be overwhelming. Some students are dealing with new varieties of temptation and negative messages from the enemy that make them feel unworthy even to approach God. Worship can afford them the opportunity to confess their sin, repent of their wrongdoings, and receive the forgiveness and restoration God wants to offer them.

5. Their sense of anxiety seeks peace.

Come to Me, all you who are weary and burdened, and I will give you rest. Take My yoke upon you and learn from Me, because I am gentle and humble in heart, and you will find rest for your souls. For My yoke is easy and My burden is light (Matt. 11:28-30).

I must admit that as a junior high or high school student, I didn't carry a calendar, Day-Timer®, or PalmPilot® to help me keep up with my schedule. That is not the case today. This generation of students is the most hurried and harried of all time. They are stressed from worries about grades, sports, teams, clubs, friends, parents, youth group, and so forth. Some are even struggling to muster the courage to be their true selves instead of accepting someone else's expectation of who they should be. They could use some peace!

What better way to experience peace than to pull aside from normal routines and distractions, either at home or at church, for some quality time with the Father and His Son? Worship gives teenagers a chance to hear the still, small voice of the Holy Spirit and infuses them with a sense of peace in the midst of a very hectic world.

6. Their sense of meaninglessness seeks purpose and fulfillment.

We know that all things work together for the good of those who love God: those who are called according to His purpose. For those He foreknew He also predestined to be conformed to the image of His Son, so that He would be the firstborn among many brothers. And those He predestined, He also called; and those He called, He also justified; those He justified, He also glorified (Rom. 8:28-30).

Purpose and meaning in life, the greatest needs of any student, can be discovered and directed through significant times of communion with God in worship. God may use a song, a sermon, a prayer, a testimony, or a quiet time of meditation to reach the heart and soul of a teenager who is seeking direction and purpose for his or her existence. It may be through times of worship that God chooses to nudge students down the path of His will for their lives.

7. Their sense of brokenness seeks healing.

This is My Servant, I strengthened Him, this is My Chosen One; I delight in Him. I have put My Spirit on Him; He will bring justice to the nations. He will not cry out or shout, or make His voice heard in the streets. He will not break a bruised reed, and he will not put out a smoldering wick (Is. 42:1-3a).

Students live in a rough world and many have been wounded physically or emotionally. They need a healing touch. Worship can help usher them into God's presence where

---

needs, my desires. The temptation is to entertain the goats at the expense of feeding the sheep.

Even a cursory reading of the Scriptures reveals a model of worship that is anything but entertaining, and can leave one saying, "Woe is me, I'm a man of unclean lips." The biblical pattern is for believers to gather for worship, inspiration, and edification and then to scatter for the work of evangelism.

Realizing that an encounter with Christ doesn't just happen and best occurs as one is intentional in this pursuit, we have taken several measures to better facilitate our students in this endeavor. For example, I go to great lengths to use sermon titles, topics, and illustrations that are timely, relevant, and applicable to students. Also, as part of the multi-generational worship experience for which we strive, I have found that expository preaching can be easily formatted into a PowerPoint® presentation. This not only offers a visual component, but we have found it to enhance the taking of notes, which is strongly encouraged from the pulpit each week.

Knowing that more information is retained through writing, as opposed to just hearing or even seeing, we provide every student with a "Life Action" notebook (8-by-5-inch three-ring binder with the church logo) for the stated purpose of storing one's sermon notes. These "Life Action" notes, found in the bulletin each week, contain the sermon outline, Scripture references, space for the writing of additional information, and a lightly shaded area at the bottom of the page, entitled "Prayerful Response." Holes are pre-punched so the insert can immediately be placed in the notebook. Many students have shared how they have later utilized these notes for both devotional and reference purposes.

During the "invitation" portion of our service, attention is drawn to the "Prayerful Response," and encouragement is given to follow through on this response both publicly and privately. The climate of our worship service lends itself to a great deal of freedom, especially during the time of invitation. One of the things I have found to be most pleasing as pastor is to see the freedom of expression our students have. They leave their seats closest to the front and regularly come to the altar and prostrate themselves in prayer.

Our experience has been that these simple elements have greatly enhanced our students' participation and, thus,

they can receive the healing and comfort only God can offer. It may be that through worship they finally understand that human effort alone cannot fix what is broken in their lives but that God is the One who can restore them to health and wholeness.[13]

Worship Settings for Students

There are a variety of church-related or church-sponsored worship experiences available to many teenagers on a regular basis. These range from the weekly Sunday morning service found in most churches to Wednesday night youth-focused gatherings to special worship times during events like camps, retreats, or DiscipleNows. Here are some of the settings where students have the opportunity to worship. Consider how student ministers can enhance the quality of these experiences for their teenagers.

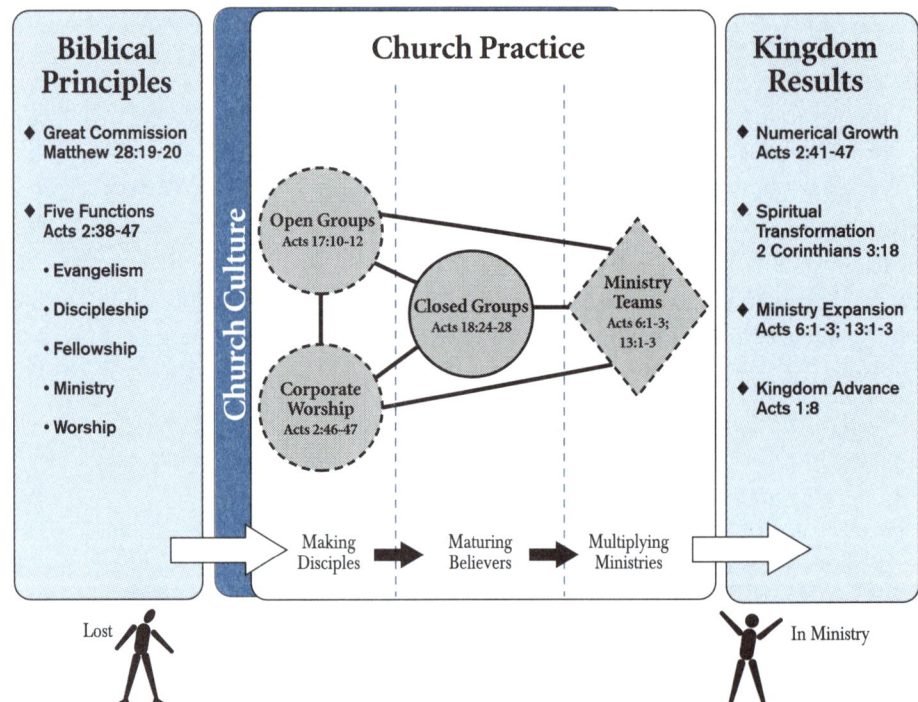

Corporate Worship (All ages)

Here we are talking about the traditional (not related to music necessarily) Sunday morning gathering in the sanctuary, worship center, auditorium, and so on, sometimes still referred to as "big church." This is one of the major elements of the MAP that can be used as a tool to discuss the church and student ministries. In this model, corporate worship is a vital contributor to the health of a kingdom-focused church—an entry point for introducing people (including teenagers) to Christ and encouraging and empowering disciples for faithful living and service.

Throughout the Old and New Testaments there are accounts of the people of God joining together for experiences of corporate worship. Could it be that such gatherings still have merit in the twenty-first century? Absolutely! Crafted in the very design of the church is the need for the body of Christ to meet together for encouragement and inspiration as it seeks to accomplish God's purposes in the world. (See Acts 2:37-47; 4:32-37; 1 Cor. 12:1–13:13.)

Perhaps it is not surprising, especially in this age of specialization, that there are so many programs and activities for students only. After all, the reasoning for doing so is to address their developmental needs appropriately and to provide programming that will be attractive to them. If we don't provide customized ministry for students, who will?

This is not faulty logic, but shouldn't it be balanced with intentional gatherings of the family of God as the family of God? Could Hebrews 10:25 be applied to the various age groups within the church? As Steven Fry has stated, "When we are in agreement before the Lord in our lives and ministries—and in our worship together—the combined effect is like that of a symphony. Together, the unique 'notes' of each life comprise an orchestra that magnifies God's glory in a way no individual can."[14] The churches' corporate worship "orchestras" need the notes of richness and joy teenage lives can offer.

Unfortunately, many students and sometimes even student ministry leaders are less than excited about participating in the corporate worship services at their churches. You've surely heard (or stated) the well-known criticisms:

"The sermons are boring."

"The music is old-fashioned."

"The worship elements and order are the same every week."

"The atmosphere in the service is cold and dry."

"Nothing about the service is relevant to my life!"

Frequently youth ministers feel powerless to address such concerns. Is there anything that can be done? Consider the following suggestions:

1. **Pray.**—Pray for your pastor, music minister, and anyone else who has a part in leading worship. Pray about talking to them concerning the form and content of the worship service. Pray for the proper spirit and attitude in which to approach them.

2. **Pray and Plan.**—Prayerfully plan the worship service with the total ministry team at your church. It may be a large staff or small, but input should be solicited from all members. We should offer our best to God through our worship and this will not happen by accident. Meaningful worship may well require more than just following the normal routine and picking out a few songs people like. The worship elements of preaching, teaching, prayer, testimony, singing and musical expression of various types, drama, video, and so forth, can be combined in profound worship, but planning will be required. There may even be avenues for students to lead in worship.

3. **Pray for and Encourage Your Pastor.**—Offer him words of encouragement on communicating with students. No one wants to see a recurrence of the "Eutychus Syndrome" (Acts 20:7-12) in our churches and you may very well be able to help your pastor with insights on youth culture as well as local teen events that could be incorporated into his messages. Daniel Aleshire reminds us, "They (teenagers) will be more likely to listen to the sermon if the preacher, without condescending, uses illustrations that reflect his awareness of the world in which they live and if the preaching occasionally addresses the problems they experience."[15]

4. **Pray and Encourage Your Students.**—You may need to help your teens see the value of gathering to worship with the entire church family. Show them Scripture that addresses this issue. Encourage them to pray for those who lead worship. Lead them to pray as they prepare to meet God in worship. Urge them to pray that God will speak specifically to them in worship and you may also want gently to remind them they are not the audience in this experience, God is. Talk about what they can offer God in their worship of Him.

---

their worship experience. In fact, our minister to youth, Jimmy Storrie, has discerned a direct correlation between those who say they "get nothing" out of the worship service and their utilization of the tools we provide for them. It seems that even in regard to worship, the old adage holds true—"You get out of it what you put into it."

—Bobby Dagnel is the pastor of the First Baptist Church of Lubbock, Texas.

For youth to learn the way of Christ they cannot and must not be segregated or isolated from the worshiping community. Youth ministry cannot be practiced with its own particular activities and methods unless they are grounded in the rhythms and presence of the community before God. This means youth must be physically recognized as equal partners in the worship of God. It is imperative that worship incorporates and makes room for the unique gifts and abilities that are present in young people.

—Mark Yaconelli, "Focusing Youth Ministry Through Christian Practices" in *Starting Right: Thinking Theologically About Youth Ministry*, Kenda Creasy Dean, Chap Clark, and Dave Rahn, eds. Grand Rapids: Zondervan Publishing House, 2001, 161.

CORPORATE WORSHIP (STUDENT WORSHIP)

It is also extremely valuable for a balanced ministry to students in a kingdom-focused church to include corporate worship experiences that are full-on, all-out designed and planned for students (funny how many of these attract adults as well, isn't it?). Freedom in the choice of worship elements and style can be very appealing to a generation of youth who desire to "experience" life in all of its facets, including those areas related to spirituality.

Another benefit of student-focused worship gatherings is that they are entry points to the church that can be used as outreach tools to students in your community. While some teenagers, especially those who have not grown up in the church, feel uncomfortable in traditional worship settings, the atmosphere of youth-focused services should be purposefully designed to make students feel both welcome and comfortable. For some students these gatherings may provide the opportunity to connect with God as they hear about Him, His magnificent attributes, and His marvelous purpose for their lives in a manner and style they can readily understand and embrace. Some settings for student-focused worship include:

> *In their spiritual quests, our young people need places where they can assemble, sing music that touches their souls, hear teaching that's relevant to them, confess their sins, bring offerings from their daily activities and eat heavenly food. And as the Good News is accepted in different youth subcultures (goths, skinheads, jocks, punks), exciting possibilities — as well as dangers — arise for youth worship. Issues of authority, form, and style confront us.*
> —Dean Borgman, "Youth Worship and the Liturgical Renewal Movement," *Youthworker,* Vol. XV No. 6 (July/August 1999); 31.

Wednesday Night Gatherings

One of the more popular venues for student-focused and student-led worship is Wednesday night. Many student ministries use this midweek meeting as their primary outreach strategy. These services often contain a good deal of music, (either by a live band or on CD), video clips from popular movies or other sources that address or introduce the night's theme, and a 15- to 30-minute teaching time. Extended times of prayer and the sharing of testimonies may also be included. Students can be involved in leading the music, creating PowerPoint® presentations and videos, speaking, praying, giving testimonies, serving as greeters, participating in dramas, leading games, running sound, and so forth.

The people who show up for these Wednesday night meetings ("Crowd") are often different (and larger) from those who show up on Sunday mornings ("Community"). That's OK; these worship times can be the entry point through which students become a part of our student ministries. The challenge will be to connect them to the other elements of our ministries (Bible study, discipleship, ministry, missions, etc.) and to the larger church family.

> *This generation wants an authentic embodiment of worship—and young people are quick and can spot a phony a mile away. But when worship is done by them—not to them or for them—they will respond.*
> —Robert Webber, "Youth Worship Q & A With the Experts," an interview in *Youthworker,* Vol. XV No. 6 (July/August 1999); 36.

Youth Camp

Whether it's Centrifuge, an associational camp, a single church camp experience, or any number of camps sponsored by youth ministry outfitters, these summer camps all include significant times of corporate worship. The added benefit of camp is that the students are outside of their normal environments and routines. Sometimes this may be what it takes for them to slow down enough to encounter God in some incredible and life-changing ways.

For many students it is in a camp setting that it finally becomes accepted to sing out loud since all their peers are doing so. They may even pray in public, offer a testimony, and express themselves to God in other ways because of the spirit of freedom and acceptance found in these services. More than likely many of us can remember significant decisions we made as teenagers at camp. It's also exciting to watch God continue to bless teenagers and adult leaders in and through these important times.

Mission Experiences

Depending on the type of mission experience, students may be involved in leading worship as a part of their mission endeavor, or they may participate in worship specifically designed for them in the course of their daily schedules. This generation of students loves to pour their hearts into significant efforts that can affect people's lives. Mission involvement that includes times of corporate worship can create a marvelous synergy of helping students meet with God in times of communion and reflection, and then serve Him in practical ways as they provide ministry to others.

Other Special Events

Retreats, DiscipleNows, student conferences, rallies, and other special events also provide opportunities to gather teenagers for worship. The worship services can range from being the focal point of the event to being a significant role-player in the overall experience. Based on the time, travel, and budget available for such events, students may be used in leadership roles, or they may get to hear from well-known speakers and musical artists.

While it is not a good idea to focus solely on events if the desire is to provide a balanced ministry to students, these events have a legitimate place in a well-rounded ministry. These special times of worship often become spiritual mile markers in students' journeys of faith. It may require advanced planning, fund raising, and loads of prayer for the events to become reality. Sometimes it seems as though one of the tasks in youth ministry is to provide opportunities for students to meet with God in some unique ways. Such events can help to accomplish this goal.

Reflection Services

As mentioned, many times God does some awesome things through student events. Let's not keep these wonderful experiences to ourselves. One way to share them with the entire church is through reflection services. These worship times can occur immediately following camp, mission trip, DiscipleNow, and so forth. Often Sunday night is an opportune time for these to take place.

Such services should be student-led and could include music, drama, video from the event, testimonies, and reports. Another effective element is to pair students with adults from the congregation at the close of the service for a time of introduction and prayer. Students can share about their recent participation in the event and tell about what they have learned or about any commitments they have made. The adults can pray with the students and pledge to be prayer partners with them as new commitments are lived out.

Personal Worship

While corporate worship services are vital to an effective student ministry, so are meaningful times of private worship. Though personal or private worship is not a part of a corporate worship strategy, it is an important aspect of the function of worship. If the only

Forming a Student Worship Team

One of the best strategies for maximum effectiveness in a local church youth ministry is connecting youth to the vision and purpose of their youth group. Having teenagers actively involved in planning and implementing youth ministry activities and programs, fulfills the mandate of "Equipping the saints for the works of ministry" in Ephesians 4. Teenagers have much to contribute to the "work" of youth ministry. One such opportunity lies in the area of worship leadership by using youth worship bands. As a functioning ministry team, youth-led worship bands will grow and develop teenagers socially, emotionally, musically, and spiritually.

Membership

If a person's greatest desire is to "fit in" or "belong," then having a team or group that teenagers can be a part of will address one or more of their greatest needs. Members of a worship team can include: singers, musicians, sound crew, video/computer/overhead projector "techies," planning team, and equipment movers (roadies). Opportunities for students young and old, outgoing and shy, creative and unimaginative, skilled and unskilled are available. There are places for students to be "up in front" and to work "behind the scenes." As a ministry team, there should be built-in levels

time our students experience worship is in large gatherings, they are missing the blessings and benefits of communing with God on a daily basis. Few things can enhance the spiritual health of teenagers more than for them to spend regular time with God in personal worship. In fact, more than likely there will be a dramatic improvement in corporate worship gatherings when students (and the adults in our churches) meet together for corporate worship after having spent a week that has included significant times of personal worship.

Jesus participated in corporate worship in the synagogue, but Scripture also reveals He consistently spent time with His Father in private worship. A few examples include His time alone with God before the calling of the disciples (Luke 4:42), before and after the feeding of the five thousand (Matt. 14:13-23), and, of course, the agonizing season of prayer in the garden of Gethsemane (Matt. 26:36-46, Mark 14:32-42, Luke 22:39-46). Christ's example of spending consistent, meaningful time with God must be our model; and, as student ministry leaders, we must set the same example for our teenagers. You've heard it before, it's impossible to lead students in a spiritual direction in which you are not headed yourself.

It is not only important to tell teenagers about the need for personal worship, but they also must be shown how to do it. A regular time of personal worship could include any number or combination of spiritual disciplines, such as:

Bible Study—close examination of the Bible under the leading of the Holy Spirit. It may focus on a book or section of Scripture, a biblical person, or a specific theme or word found in Scripture.

Contemplation—quiet time to reflect on your walk with Christ and His love for you. It may include coming face-to-face with areas of sin and determining ways your life should be different.

Journaling—tracking your relationship with God. It includes recording prayers, words you hear from God, prayer requests for others, insights from Scripture, and verses you want to remember. It may also include poetry, drawings, quotations, diagrams, stories, or written reflections.

Meditation—Christian meditation often means choosing a passage of Scripture to contemplate and seeking to understand totally what God is telling you through it.

Prayer—much more than saying grace at every meal. It involves quickly raising every issue of your life to God as they occur.

Scripture Memory—consistently committing God's Word to memory so it is available to you for worship or spiritual warfare.

Silence—the discipline of closing out all distractions for a time. Is there ever a time in your life when all the noise is turned off?[16]

Times of personal worship can also include music, whether it is through singing, playing an instrument, or just listening to a favorite worship CD. Employing a variety of these spiritual disciplines can help keep private times of worship fresh. Most of all, these times will be opportunities for adult leaders and their students to grow closer to God as they speak to Him through prayers and songs of praise, and listen to Him through His Word in the counsel of the Holy Spirit.

Usually the bulk of private worship is spent in prayer and Bible study. It can be helpful to share with students a plan or process for how this time could be spent. Here is a suggested outline for how one might spend this time.

1. **Pray.**—Ask God to reveal His thoughts to you as you read His Word.
2. **Read.**—Read God's Word. Many devotional plans are available, but the best resource is God's own Word. Most devotional books structure the daily thoughts so each page begins with a passage of Scripture on which the devotional thought is based. Read His Word first.
3. **Journal.**—Write down what God says to you in His Word. Writing is a helpful discipline because it helps articulate what we discovered from our reading and prayers.
4. **Pray again.**—This time write down your prayer. Let it reflect what you have discovered out of His communication to you.
5. **Write an application statement.**—This may be the most difficult thing you do. In your journal, be as specific as possible about what you will do with what you have discovered. (A change of attitude, or an action you will take, for example.)
6. **Read the devotional thought.**—See if what you discovered from God's Word is the same as what the devotional writer discovered. Most of the time you and the writer will come up with different messages. It may be that God wants to show you something different from His Word.
7. **Pray.**—Close out your time with God by praying about the whole process. Did He tell you that you needed to change a relationship, confess a sin, or correct a wrong? Ask for His strength to accomplish what He desires.[17]

One of the greatest challenges to personal worship is the issue of time. People are busy. Teenagers are busy. The reality is that time is required for any relationship to grow and develop; yet again, Jesus is the example. As He came to the close of His earthly life, He was able to say He had accomplished everything the Father had sent Him to do (John 17:4). What an incredible statement at the close of one's life. As busy as Jesus was, especially during His public ministry, He was still able to have regular times of personal worship with the Father.

You can encourage your students to be faithful in their personal worship by providing devotional guides and books, journals, worship CDs, and other resources. Encourage them to develop relationships of accountability regarding their devotional lives. In addition, you may want to include opportunities in your programming for students to share what they have been learning and experiencing in their times alone with God.

FAMILY WORSHIP

Meaningful times of praise, prayer, Bible study, and encouragement also can occur in the setting of family worship. This could include brief devotionals over a meal or designated gatherings where each family member is responsible for a different worship element. Much like personal worship, these times of worship will not happen by accident. They will require both planning and commitment. As youth leaders, we can help facilitate family worship by designing and distributing family worship guides. By doing so we can support

---

of accountability and expectations (covenants are a good idea). Formally enlisting or auditioning all of the ministry team members could prove to be very helpful. Younger singers and musicians can serve in the "behind the scenes" positions as they watch and learn from older teenagers and adults. Involving volunteer adults with musical background and experience is very wise. They can mentor teenagers in playing instruments, using equipment, and vocal techniques, all in the context of a ministry setting. If there are openings or gaps in the band, use these adults to minister alongside the students.

A key ingredient in forming this ministry team involves the "team building" process. Begin forming/enlisting team members several months before using them. This lengthy formation time allows opportunities for group building and "band chemistry." A weekend retreat to begin this process will be time well-spent. Band members and vocalists need to be able to count on the support, encouragement, and stability of a "tight knit" group (not just musically, but emotionally as well).

DISCIPLESHIP

Opportunities for the spiritual growth and maturity of band members are plentiful. Daily quiet times, pre-service devotional/prayer times, and other topical Bible studies can be incorporated as a part of a covenant or weekly accountability requirements. As part of the formation process, several sessions of group Bible study on worship and servant-leadership can lay the foundation for the direction and focus of the worship team. Weekly pre-service prayer times can aid in group building; but more importantly they will be spiritually affirming and uplifting. Examining and understanding the message and theology of song lyrics provide significant teachable moments. Some rehearsals should be spent just in facilitating worship for students and adults on this ministry team. Team members may struggle to worship as they lead, work, and serve. Students should be grounded and challenged to grow not only musically, but also spiritually in moments of Bible study, explanation, prayer, and personal worship.

SOME FINAL THOUGHTS... BE CAREFUL!

There are a plethora of reasons (some good, some bad) for teenagers to indicate interest in being part of a worship band. The leader of this ministry team needs to be able to discern the motives and potential of each member.

families and encourage parents who are seeking to enhance the spiritual lives of their teens through hands-on involvement in their lives (Deut. 6:4-9).

Leading Students in Worship

One of the exciting things about student-focused worship is teaching teenagers about worship as we lead them and involve them in leading in worship. Youth leaders can help to facilitate authentic worship for their students no matter the size of the group or the quality of the facility or resources. The foundation for worship planning and preparation must be prayer and an uncompromising reliance on the Holy Spirit. In terms of practical considerations, Lance Howerton, managing director of Student Events at LifeWay offers the following suggestions for worship leaders:

1. **Build your team.**—From leaders to greeters to sound and video technicians, everyone will need to be on the same page and aware of the goal you are trying to accomplish each week.
2. **Get them trained.**—More than enlisting warm bodies, part of our presenting an offering of worship worthy for our God is to do it to the best of our ability. Training is imperative.
3. **Make your worship a quality experience.**—Strive for the service to be a quality time with God. Today's students will expect our best and our Lord deserves nothing less.
4. **Use your students to lead worship (See sidebar beginning on p.94.).**—Worship teams provide a wonderful opportunity for students to use a variety of gifts and abilities to serve God. A student worship team is a great example of a ministry team from the MAP model.
5. **Avoid holes in worship.**—Timing should be crisp. Pay attention to the flow of the service so there will be a minimum of distractions.
6. **Practice! Practice! Practice!**—This is vital for everyone involved.
7. **Cue tapes, CD's, video and check your overheads or PowerPoint® slides.**—How many times have you witnessed an embarrassing situation in worship because these things weren't checked out beforehand? Be sure everything is working before the service begins!
8. **Have written orders of worship.**—This will help all of those leading worship to see how each element fits together and will help to eliminate surprises.
9. **Pre-worship prayer time.**—This helps the worship team focus on God and the reason for worship.
10. **Start and end on time.**—This lets students know it will be important for them to arrive on time so they don't miss any part of the service. It also will communicate to their parents you are sensitive to the demands on their time and the time of their teens.
11. **Delegate! Delegate! Delegate!**—Don't try to do everything yourself. Allow others to use their giftedness. You need to see yourself as the person who gets it done, not the person who does it.[18]

LEADING VS. PERFORMING

A word of caution. Whether it is our students, or us as worship leaders, we must be careful not to fall in the trap of worship becoming performance. This will require spiritual maturity and sensitivity to the Holy Spirit. Putting ourselves or our students in front of others, especially on a platform, can become quite a heady experience.

Matt Redman speaks of the value of being an "unnoticed" worshiper. He mentions the story of the poor widow from Luke 21:1-4 as a prime example. As he reminds us, "first God seeks devotion to Him in the hidden place—worship when no one else is watching."[19] Matt goes on to offer this challenge to worship leaders:

The really hard part begins when we start getting trusted with the public stuff. Maybe that means playing in the worship team at church or wherever. God calls us to ruthlessly check the motives of our hearts. Do we still want to be unnoticed worshipers now that we're on stage? Or is there a part of us that really wants to be noticed worshipers?…Are our songs still aimed at an audience of one, or deep down are we starting to want wider acclaim?[20]

These are some serious questions, but we need to wrestle with them as we contemplate proper motives within our worship leadership. Worship leader Chris Tomlin echoes this sentiment when he said, "Hopefully I'm not leading people to myself, because in the end if they're drawn to me, to my personality, that's going to last about a weekend. Hopefully I'm leading them to God."[21]

ENERGY VS. EMOTIONALISM

A second word of caution involves the issue of adolescent emotions when it comes to worship. As we plan and lead in worship experiences for students, it will be worthwhile to pay attention to the emotional climate we set in worship. High-energy services are attractive to teens, and certainly we have much to celebrate as we praise our God. The caution would be not to over-emphasize emotion or in any way manipulate the emotions of our students in hopes of eliciting a certain type of response from them.

This may be particularly valuable at special events like camps, retreats, DiscipleNows, and other multiple-day events where student fatigue becomes as issue. While teenagers are no strangers to experiencing a wide range of emotions, often in a very short time, this tendency increases when they are physically, mentally, and emotionally worn out.

Additionally, avoid the trap of teaching students they must "feel" a certain way in order to have worshiped. To do so may put unrealistic expectations in their minds and cause them to seek the emotional "fix" a certain style of worship service may provide. The challenge will be to seek a balance in helping them focus their hearts and minds on encountering God with the enthusiasm that is naturally present in teenagers. Blending authentic worship with young hearts on fire for God can produce some amazing results.

A Lifestyle of Worship

Paul said in Romans 12 that true worship involves a complete sacrifice of our lives to God. This must be the ultimate goal of our worship. It involves far more than a service or a style of music. It is a lifestyle of surrender to our Lord.

This also should be our goal for the students God has entrusted to us in ministry. We must make sure the worship experiences we plan lead students to opportunities for life change. Such experiences, whether corporate, private, or with their families, can help them renew their minds and point them in the direction of God's will for their lives.

Trust and respect given to youth leaders can be quickly eradicated by placing a student in a position where he or she is embarrassed or humiliated. Rehearsing (preparation) is a key factor to ensure students are ready to play and sing. New music takes time to learn and master.

BE INTENTIONAL!

A purpose statement or mission statement helps students know the philosophy and ministry objective of the band from the start. These are great enlistment tools for youth, their parents, and participating adults. Use the newly formed ministry team to create a covenant or accountability agreement. Communicating clearly the intention and purpose of the band will protect the leaders and students from misunderstandings.

Defining parameters on who is eligible to participate on this ministry team will be very helpful. Age, skill, spiritual pilgrimage, and instrumentation all need to be determined ahead of time. The size and age of the youth group, musical and sound equipment available, and the meeting space will determine the size and scope of the ministry team (how many, how loud, how much budget).

BE PRAYERFUL!

Praying for youth and adults who would support and staff this ministry team is the beginning point for ministry success. "Listen" and "watch" for teenagers and adults who act interested and are vocal about this kind of ministry. Ask God to lead you to (and lead to you), the right people as you begin the enlistment process. Ask God for creativity and flexibility in formatting this ministry team to work in your setting.

—Scott Lane is the minister to students at the First Baptist Church of San Antonio, Texas.

---

[1] Louie Giglio, "Worship—It's What We Do", accessed at *www.passion.org*.
[2] Franklin Segler, *Christian Worship; It's Theology and Practice,* Nashville: Broadman Press, 1967, p. 4-12.
[3] Ibid., p. 6-10.
[4] Adapted from Segler, p. 86-90.
[5] Ron Owens with Jan McMurray, *Return to Worship,* Nashville: Broadman & Holman, 1999, p.92-98.
[6] Wesley L. Forbis, Editor, Introduction to *The Baptist Hymnal,* Nashville: Convention Press, 1991, p. vi.
[7] Matt Redman, *The Unquenchable Worshiper: Coming Back to the Heart of Worship,* Ventura: Regal, 2001 p. 57-8.
[8] Barna Research, "Focus on 'Worship Wars' Hides the Real Issue Regarding Connection to God," 19 November 2002. [Cited 17 February 2003] Available from the Internet: *www.barna.org*. Used by permission.
[9] Ibid.
[10] Walt Harrah in Anne Ortlund, *Up with Worship: How to Quit Playing Church,* Nashville: Broadman & Holman, 2001, p.11.
[11] Elmer Towns, *Putting an End to Worship Wars,* Nashville: Broadman & Holman, 1997, p. 3.
[12] Ibid., p. 61.
[13] Adapted from Segler, p. 84-86.
[14] Steven Fry, "Beyond Lone-Ranger Worship," *Discipleship Journal,* Vol. 22, No. 6 (Nov/Dec 2002): 53.
[15] Daniel O. Aleshire, *Faithcare: Ministering to All God's People Through the Ages of Life,* Philadelphia: Westminster Press, 1988, p. 139-40.
[16] Julie Hunt, "Disciplines Defined – Truth Paper 3" in *Vital Truth: How Can I Stay Close to God?*, Nashville: LifeWay Press, 2002.
[17] Chuck Gartman and Richard Barnes, *Youth Sunday School for a New Century*, Nashville: LifeWay Press, 1999, p. 44-45.
[18] Lance Howerton, *The Centrifuge Guide to Youth Worship,* Nashville: Convention Press, 1999, p. 95-100.
[19] Redman, p. 85.
[20] Ibid., p. 87.
[21] Leslie McKellar, "Profile: Chris Tomlin," *Christian Single,* Vol. 24, No. 11 (Feb. 2003): 15.

Basic Student Ministry

chapter 6

ADMINISTRATION

Richard Ross

"AFTER A SHOOTER ATTACKED OUR YOUTH group, I now have a desire to live each day as if it could be my last. I believe God has created each of His children with different strengths and spiritual gifts—including teenagers. I really do believe it will be us who will lead the church—and society—into revival. It isn't age that matters, but the heart."

—Rebecca, 15
Fort Worth, Texas

What leaders do in response to the call of God on our lives and His commissioning us to serve His churches is the most important thing we have to do in our lives. How we lead and what we accomplish literally means spiritual life and death to millions of people on earth. Our resolve to lead churches in making disciples, maturing them, and putting them into kingdom ministries is the central focus of our lives because it is the central focus of the kingdom of God. Nothing is more important than our correct response to His call and agenda.
—Gene Mims, Vice President, LifeWay Church Resources

Planning

Signs abound that God may be raising up teenagers to lead His church into revival. Here is a question I often ask youth ministry students in my seminary classroom: "If you really thought this might be the next revival generation, how would that change how you plan youth ministry?"

God is sovereign and there is nothing leaders can do to coerce Him into doing anything. Youth ministers cannot orchestrate His coming in revival, but wise leaders raise the sails for revival in their ministries. Then, if Sovereign God sends the winds of revival, those youth ministries—likes ships of old—will move swiftly wherever God wills.

For some youth ministers, planning is boring, boring is bad, and bad is to be avoided. Not only does planning seem boring, but it is done on most youth ministers' weak side of the brain. The majority are stronger in creativity and personal relationships than administration. For them, planning never will happen naturally.

Youth ministers should erase from their minds that planning youth ministry is a cold, administrative function—not with a possible revival generation in the wings. As Henry

Blackaby has made clear, what leaders call planning can be seen simply as discovering where God is at work and joining Him there. If we sense God is at work on school campuses, we join Him there as we establish equal access clubs. If we sense He is repairing broken families, we expand our ministry with parents and families of youth.

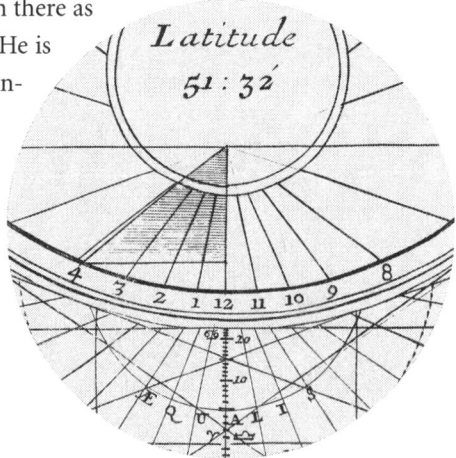

Planning answers the questions; "If Jesus chaired our team planning meetings, where would He lead us to work?" "What would be His priorities?" "What events would He design to put on the calendar?" There is nothing boring about that.

The Flow of Planning

High quality planning for youth ministry has eight distinct steps:
1. Craft a mission statement.
2. Organize a core planning team.
3. Determine the strengths and weaknesses of current ministry, and watch for where God is already at work.
4. Guide the core planning team to choose priorities based on strengths and weaknesses.
5. Guide the core planning team to set goals.
6. Guide the core planning team to choose programming and ministries most likely to meet those goals.
7. Move the programming and ministries selected to the master calendar.
8. Organize ministry teams, often called lead teams, to accept ultimate responsibility for carrying out the events and ministries on the master calendar.

Youth Ministry Mission Statements

Once, youth leaders believed there was inherent value in keeping teenagers busy. They honestly thought they could save the young from harm by filling most of their waking hours with activity. Leaders put in 70-hour work weeks to over-program teenagers so that they couldn't find time to sin.

For years (even decades) many youth ministers have walked into core planning team meetings and asked, "Well, what do ya'll want to do?" Any activity that sounded like a somewhat positive way to spend time usually ended up on the youth calendar.

Mature youth leaders do not buy that approach anymore. They have spent too many years watching teenagers who came to every activity—until they had to start staying home with their new baby or they could not get out of juvenile detention to attend.

Mature youth leaders are tired of activity for activity's sake. They are tired of the toll it takes on themselves and their families. They are tired of questioning whether what they do has lasting value. It is past time for churches in general, and youth ministries specifically, to become intentional about everything they do. The times demand it. Everything done must become kingdom-focused because:

Basic Student Ministry

- There is no evidence that busyness alone leads to salvation, discipleship, or even a moral lifestyle.
- There is not enough money to do everything. Churches do not have it and families do not have it.
- There is not enough time to do it all. Volunteer leaders, even the committed ones, have finite time to give. Teenagers over-programmed by schools, teams, and jobs cannot or will not do it all either.
- The charge to win this generation to Jesus Christ demands that every action taken be strategic and targeted.

Writing mission statements marks an important step toward intentional youth ministry. Small churches with a handful of youth and mega churches with thousands will benefit from the discipline of getting their direction down on paper.

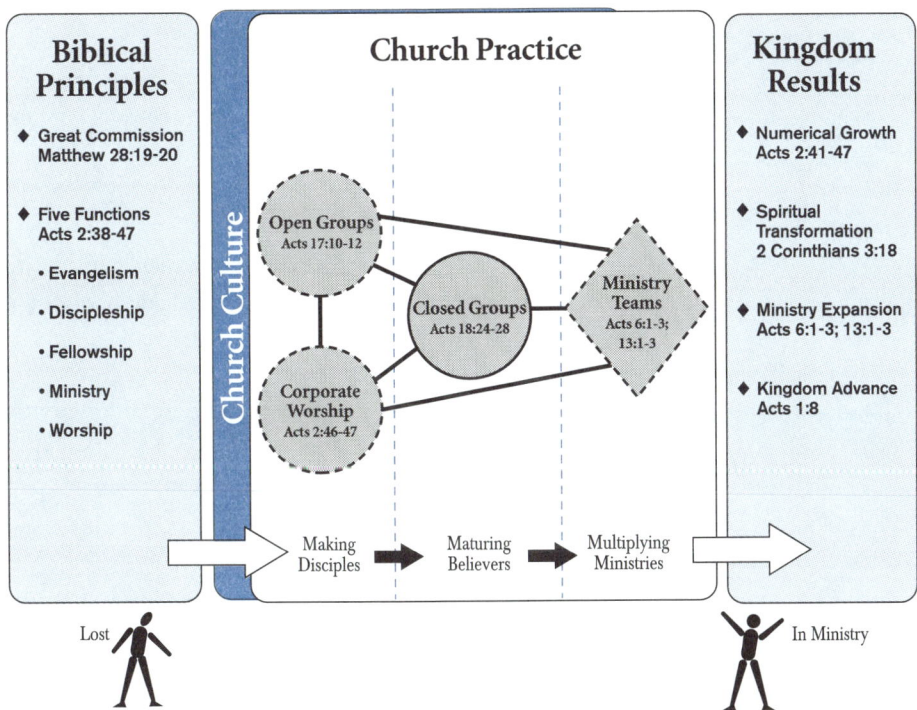

Overview of Mission Statements

Doug Fields has noted, "I have seen an obvious relationship between spiritual and numerical growth in youth ministries that have discovered the five … (biblical functions) purposes, defined them in a clear statement, and put leadership behind the purposes."[1] Every church, large and small, should move toward a written mission statement.

A mission statement is a restatement of the Great Commission in contemporary terms the church can embrace. It is a concise sentence or sentences that explains why a church's youth ministry exists. It is the final answer to the question, Why do we do what we do? (The terms *purpose statement* and *mission statement* can be used interchangeably.) Note the central place of the Great Commission in defining a youth ministry's mission in the MAP diagram. (See chart.) A good mission statement is:

- **Aligned**—Every mission statement should be aligned with the pastor's leadership and direction of the church.
- **Proactive**—A kingdom-focused youth ministry takes the initiative to act, not react. All youth ministries face external threats and challenges. It is OK to acknowledge those, but the focus in a mission statement should be on taking responsibility for moving forward.
- **Principle-Centered**—There are plenty of community organizations that want to provide something positive for teenagers. The local church is unique only if it is squarely centered on principles of Scripture.
- **Adaptable**—Every youth ministry group, class, or ongoing program should be able to adapt the mission statement to their particular work.
- **Simple**—It should be short enough for new teenagers to memorize, yet long enough to be complete.
- **Broad**—It should be broad enough to be comprehensive for the organization.
- **Understandable**—It should be understandable even by younger teenagers and parents of teenagers outside the church.

George Barna's study of contemporary Christian teenagers reveals they are hungry for vision and purpose. They will be attracted to a youth ministry that knows where it is going and why. They don't recoil from too great a challenge, but from too little.[2]

The Church's Mission Statement

In an ideal world, leaders in youth ministry take the church's mission statement as the starting point in writing statements for their youth ministry. The mission of every subministry of a church should be a targeted reflection of the church's overarching direction.

For example, consider these mission statements from Willow Creek Community Church and Saddleback Valley Community Church.

Willow Creek Community Church—"The mission of WCCC is to turn irreligious people into fully devoted followers of Jesus Christ."

Willow Creek High School Ministry.—"The mission of Student Impact is to turn irreligious high school students into fully devoted followers of Jesus Christ."

Saddleback Valley Community Church—"To bring people to Jesus and membership in His family, develop them to Christlike maturity, and equip them for their ministry in the church and life mission in the world, in order to magnify God's name."

Saddleback Youth Ministry—"To reach non-believing students, to connect them with other Christians, to help them grow in their faith, and to challenge the growing to discover their ministry and honor God with their lives."

In the real world, the great majority of churches have not defined their mission. Some youth ministers may have the privilege of motivating the pastor and key church leaders to move in this direction if they are initially uninterested in establishing the church's mission.

Writing Mission Statements

A very small group should work with the youth minister on the first draft of mission statements. Even a core planning team may be too large for this task. Dream consolidation and wordsmithing are just too difficult with a large group.

The handful of adults who work on the first draft should be the church's core youth ministry leaders. They need to feel a call and commitment to youth ministry and have a heart for God and commitment to the overall mission of the local church.

Crafting mission statements is hard work and can be time-consuming. Churches may or may not choose to include youth in this initial work. A teenager will need unusual spiritual maturity and discipline to perform in this role.

After a small group has prepared the first draft, proposed mission statements should be shared with concentric circles of the youth ministry family. This pattern will vary from church to church. A sample pattern might include sharing the first draft with:

1. Pastor and other ministers on staff
2. Core planning team
3. All church-elected youth leaders
4. The entire youth ministry family

The core leaders who draft the first statements must consider any proposed changes carefully. Certainly, feedback from ministers and the core planning team, if well-thought-out, may lead to revisions. In the larger meetings, changes only should be made if there is broad consensus and a sense that God is speaking. The vision of the youth minister, and the long and hard work of the initial writing group, should not be abandoned flippantly.

Communicating and Implementing the Mission Statement

Once mission statements are adopted by the youth ministry family, they become the driving force in everything done. "Keeping your ministry purpose-driven will help you avoid becoming action- or activity-oriented, rather than Christ-centered and focused."[3]

The hard work of writing mission statements is lost unless they are communicated in the everyday life of youth ministry. Rick Warren, senior pastor at Saddleback Valley Community Church notes, "Once you have defined the purposes of your church, you must continually clarify and communicate them to everyone in your congregation. It is not a task you do once and then forget about. This is the foremost responsibility of leadership. If you fail to communicate your statement of purpose to your members, you may as well not have one."[4] In youth ministry, this might mean:

1. Printing the mission statements at the bottom of all youth calendars or newsletters.
2. Placing the statements on permanent signs in the room where core planning team meetings are held.
3. Printing the statements on place mats at a leadership banquet.
4. Hanging banners with the statements in the youth area.
5. Offering rewards at events to youth who can quote the statements from memory.
6. Teaching on the mission statements.
7. Placing the statements on letters going to parents and new youth leaders.

The Youth Minister's Role in Setting the Mission

The youth minister (or volunteer coordinator) is the key to this process. His or her calling and passion for the future will be at the heart of written statements.

He or she also is the catalyst in consolidating shared dreams. Few churches have a clear direction for youth ministry until a youth minister leads them in that direction. When it comes to drawing out dreams, the youth minister is similar to an early American butter maker. The youth minister:

1. Agitates the milk in the churn
   - Calls meetings of core youth and leaders
   - Gently jars them to think carefully about mission

Administration

- Lifts up intimacy with God and God's written revelation as central to the dreaming process
- Shares his or her own heart, passion, and view of the future
2. Skims off the butter as it rises
    - Listens carefully for dreams to emerge from core youth, adult leaders, and parents
    - Realizes dreams seldom emerge fully formed, so he affirms and gathers even pieces of dreams
3. Packages the butter
    - Guides the initial writing team to consolidate shared dreams into concrete mission statements

THE YOUTH MINISTER'S PERSONAL PHILOSOPHY OF YOUTH MINISTRY

The youth minister does assist a church in consolidating and defining its mission and purpose. That is not to say he or she only guides the process. The personal ministry philosophy of the youth minister is front and center all through the process. The final mission statement and the shape of ministry for that church will carry the thumbprints of the youth minister. Value and belief statements adopted by Southern Baptist Convention and state associate youth workers in the 2003 Youth Summit can be found in Appendix 4. It might serve as a beginning point for others just starting to define a similar statement.

CREATING A CORE PLANNING TEAM

No youth minister working alone can match the effectiveness he or she would experience dreaming and planning with key members of the youth ministry team. Here are several advantages of planning youth ministry with some type of core planning team (In many churches these are called the youth council, youth committee, youth core planning team.).

- **Working with a core planning team shows respect for the abilities of teenagers.**—Certainly teenagers are not adults and should not be expected consistently to exhibit adult characteristics, but they are not children either. Teenagers have growing abilities that need to be affirmed by the church. Churches that do not involve teenagers in key planning roles may appear archaic to young people.
- **Working with a core planning team shows respect for the thoughts and abilities of adult leaders and parents.**—Without intending to, youth ministers can communicate the following messages to the church.
  - Adult leaders are out of touch with teenagers. The church must look to me alone for insights about youth.
  - Adult leaders will not make the time commitments ministry requires. The church can only count on me to get the job done.
  - Adult leaders are basically boring. I am the only one with creativity and workable ideas.

    Involving key adults in planning youth ministry communicates just the opposite of these messages. It says to the church the youth minister has formed a partnership with adult leaders and parents based on mutual respect.
- **A core planning team can utilize teenager's insights into the needs and interests of their age group.**—Youth are also authorities on the interests of other teenagers. Planning performed only by adults will occasionally miss the mark. Planning that involves representative teenagers can be more consistently on target.

- **A core planning team allows members to feel ownership of youth ministry.**—If the youth minister conceives, promotes, and implements ministry plans alone, teenagers will consider those plans "the youth minister's thing." Youth may or may not choose to participate, depending on their moods at the moment. They will feel little personal concern about whether the plans succeed or fail.

Teenagers involved in all phases of planning and implementing youth ministry will sense, "This is our thing." Teenagers who feel ownership of an event will work hard to make it successful.

Certainly, it is not possible for every teenager to be directly involved in planning every youth event. The fact that youth serve on a core planning team (and lead teams) will create a mentality among the entire group that *youth ministry is ours*.

The same principle is true of adult leaders and parents. Youth ministers who exclude leaders and parents from the dreaming and planning of ministry events may wonder why they are so "uncommitted" or "unsupportive" when it comes time to do the work. Adults as well as teenagers will give surprising effort to directions and ministries that are theirs.

Choosing a Planning Cycle

Once key youth, adult leaders, and parents come together to form a core planning team, planning can begin. First, the youth minister and the team must decide how far into the future to plan. Generally, teams plan either one month, one quarter, or one year ahead.

A. Monthly—Some churches plan their youth calendars one month at a time. Toward the end of one month they begin to think through what they would like to do the following month. This approach has some weaknesses:
- Making reservations for facilities, transportation, or guest leaders in a timely manner is difficult.
- Building continuity through the year is more difficult.
- Allowing lead teams to do the actual work of preparing for events is almost impossible.
- Helping families protect dates for future youth trips or activities is difficult.
- Choosing programming based on strengths and weaknesses seldom happens.
- Designing events based on stated goals and priorities is rare.

Churches doing monthly planning should consider moving to an annual, or at the very least quarterly, planning process. Taking this step almost will guarantee more effective ministry.

B. Quarterly—Quarterly planning is an improvement over monthly planning, but still suffers from some of the weaknesses noted above. A wise youth minister will slowly guide the core planning team to move to an annual planning process.

A good intermediate step in that direction involves planning all major events on an annual basis and then filling in the details on smaller events on a quarterly basis. For example, the team could make a decision on an out-of-state mission trip a year ahead, but plan an after-worship recreation event a quarter ahead.

This hybrid of annual and quarterly planning may be especially practical in a church that does no overall annual planning. It is a little frustrating to make complete youth ministry plans for a year, then to see churchwide events and emphases layered on top of those dates as the year unfolds.

Administration

In this instance, the core planning team might annually propose major dates to the senior pastor and those who plan with him. With a cooperative spirit, the youth minister might say, "Pastor, here are some dates for some major youth trips and events for the year. We need to make financial commitments in some cases and begin the planning process for those events to be effective. Do you think these dates will fit into the overall church calendar, and could you do what you can to protect these dates in the planning process?"

Once the major dates are set, then the planning team can fill in smaller events as the overall church calendar emerges each quarter. A minimum goal would be to have everything nailed down a full month before a new quarter begins.

C. Annually—Annual planning may seem daunting to inexperienced youth ministers, but it is a skill well worth developing. It offers many advantages:
- Presenting to the youth ministry family a full year of ministry events builds excitement and commitment.
- Knowing what you will do all year long makes budget proposals easy to develop.
- Having a year's head start makes it possible to reserve the best facilities, enlist the most effective leaders, and get the lowest rates.
- Knowing the major events of the year enables parents to choose vacations and other family commitments that don't conflict.
- Planning a year in advance gives lead teams plenty of time to do their work without going into a crisis planning mode.

Certainly, annual planning is done in broad strokes. For example, after annual planning the youth minister will know:
- A parent and youth retreat will be held April 19-20.
- The primary goal will be to train families in how to resolve conflict without damaging each other.

The youth minister may not know:
- Who will lead the retreat.
- What will be the agenda for the retreat.
- What will be served for Friday dinner.

The youth minister will know:
- Youth will participate in local service projects that directly confront human needs.
- The projects will be planned for the first Wednesday evening of each month.

The youth minister may not know:
- Where those monthly projects will be conducted.

Annual planning lays out the broad plan for the year. Detailed planning continues all year.

RELATIONSHIP TO CHURCH PLANNING
Relating the youth calendar to the church calendar is no easy process. Here are basic facts.
1. If the church has defined mission statements, then youth ministry mission statements should flow from them. This means youth plans that support youth ministry mission statements also will support the church's mission.

Basic Student Ministry

2. If the church sets priorities and goals for the year, then the youth ministry calendar should support them.

What is unclear is the process for meshing the annual planning process when it comes down to actual events and programming. Churches approach this one of two ways.

Church Calendar First

In some churches, the church planning process is limited to churchwide events. Once the church leadership team has completed this process, then age-group ministries (such as youth ministry) and other programs and ministries are free to do annual planning for events and emphases unique to their target audiences. Each ministry builds its calendar around the adopted churchwide calendar.

A youth minister (or volunteer coordinator) assembles the core planning team after the church leadership team has completed their annual planning process. The team is basically free to develop its own annual plan, consistent with the overall goals of the church and not in conflict with churchwide events or emphases.

Church Calendar Last

In other churches, age groups and ministries in the church are charged to develop proposed calendars for the new year. Then, representatives from those ministries come together with the church leadership team (may be the church council in some churches) to hammer out a final church calendar.

A youth minister assembles the core planning team before the church leadership team begins its work. The team must complete its tentative calendar for presentation to the churchwide body.

A brand new staff minister or coordinator quickly should learn how the church plans, so he or she can adjust the youth ministry planning schedule accordingly. There is no healthy or effective alternative but to mesh with the church process.

The Planning Process

The core planning team moves through five steps in planning the annual, quarterly, or monthly youth calendar. The steps are logical, practical, and in proper sequence. Together they make it very likely every activity and event is directly related to accomplishing an important ministry goal and impacting a target audience.

STEP 1—EXAMINE STRENGTHS AND WEAKNESSES

The core planning team should begin by looking closely at strengths and weaknesses in the church's ministry to youth. Needs faced by teenagers, youth parents, and adult leaders all are valid concerns of the team. Planning cannot be based on strengths and needs unless they clearly are in focus all through the planning process. The team can gather feedback by:
 1. Administering and interpreting published survey forms;
 2. Creating, administering, and interpreting original survey forms;
 3. Hosting a "Town Hall Meeting" of all youth, parents, and leaders designed to garner feedback;
 4. Reviewing progress made toward reaching goals from the previous year;

Step 2—Select Several Priority Issues

The first step will reveal more strengths and weaknesses than can be addressed during one period of time. The second step, selecting several priority issues, becomes vital. Enough resources generally are not available to address every issue at the same time.

The issues chosen in step 2 should be chosen from the strengths and weaknesses defined in step 1. An exception might be priorities that grow out of a churchwide emphasis or plan for the year.

The youth ministry's mission statement should guide the core planning team in choosing priority issues. The mission statement visually should be before the group during this step and the youth minister should make reference to it from time to time.

One or two priority issues should be selected for each youth ministry function as discussed in each of the previous chapters: evangelism, discipleship, fellowship, ministry, and worship.

Priorities also should be selected in view of the specific audiences that will be targeted for ministry moving students from making, maturing, and multiplying as discussed in chapter 2 in the "Crowd", "Group", "Committed", or "Multiplier" groups.

Step 3—Set Goals

Goals are those clearly defined areas of work toward which youth ministry will move. Goals need to be observable and measurable. Each goal should have some objective way to determine if it has been achieved by the end of the planning cycle.

Writing measurable goals is hard work. Some may want to skip this step. Teams that discipline themselves, however, to write clear goals will be rewarded with focused plans. Because these goals will determine the entire direction of the church's youth ministry, the goals should be selected with care and after much prayer.

You should not have more goals than priorities. Five to ten goals should be considered a maximum. If two priorities can be covered in one goal, so much the better. Most goals will fall under the categories mentioned in the introduction: numerical growth, spiritual transformation, ministry expansion, and kingdom advance.

Step 4—Choose Programming and Ministries

In an earlier era of youth ministry, this was the first step. The first order of business for many councils and committees was just to think of things to do. It should now be apparent how much stronger it is to think of programming only after strengths and needs have been defined, priority areas chosen, and clear goals established.

The best way to achieve worthy goals is to provide a series of high-quality events, emphases, and ministries designed to provide youth ministry experiences in the areas of the goals. The challenging part is coming up with the original ideas.

The youth minister and core planning team must not become preoccupied with major events and fail to give careful attention to ongoing, weekly ministries. Weekly ministries that impact youth, adult leaders, or parents almost 52 weeks of the year can be powerful tools for achieving youth ministry goals. Strategic planning related to those ministries deserves just as careful attention as do major events. Note that corporate worship, open groups, closed groups, and ministry teams (see MAP) represent primary, ongoing strategies for accomplishing youth ministry goals.

Calendar Minimums

Of course, there is no "universal law" about what should make up a youth ministry; each church has to find its own way. Smaller churches with limited resources might at least consider the following to be a minimum level of programming.

1. One or two weekly opportunities for corporate worship with the entire church.
2. An ongoing program (ideally each week) that involves youth, adult leaders, and perhaps parents in sharing their faith and reaching out to lost youth and their parents.
3. A weekly, open group Bible teaching and reaching organization that begins with the biblical revelation and moves toward life application.
4. A weekly, closed discipleship group targeted to Christian youth who desire deeper discipleship content, lifestyle and attendance accountability, and study/spiritual preparation between meetings.
5. An ongoing ministry team that helps youth develop a heart for missions and involves them in direct missions service.
6. A weekly music experience targeted to youth who feel called to minister and worship through their musical gifts. In smaller churches this could include adults.
7. Occasional youth-focused worship experiences targeted to all youth.
8. A monthly, major event designed to accomplish one or more important youth ministry goals and impact one or more of the target audiences of youth.
9. A few events each quarter designed to build relationships and fellowship within the youth ministry family (youth, adult leaders, or parents).
10. A biannual event designed to assist parents of youth in their parenting roles.
11. An annual event designed to inspire and equip all adults who minister with youth.
12. A time and place for teenagers to pray together, either during or outside the weekly youth organizations.

Those elements represent a practical minimum, even in the smallest churches. If there are one youth leader, two teenagers, and two parents, they can have the experiences listed above. By periodically joining with other churches and by participating in larger youth ministry events, even smaller churches can have rich experiences beyond their own church campus.

STEP 5—CREATE THE YOUTH MINISTRY CALENDAR

At this point, programming elements selected in step 4 should be placed on the calendar. Here are several principles:

1. Try to create rhythm and flow throughout the year, avoiding periods with too much activity and periods with nothing to do.
2. Space out events that are financially expensive to families.
3. Coordinate the church youth ministry calendar with school and community calendars.
    A. Order school calendars as soon as the school board adopts them in the spring.
    B. Order football and other team calendars as soon as they are adopted.
    C. Order a calendar of community events from the Chamber of Commerce.
4. Coordinate the youth ministry calendar with the full church calendar.

Administration

A. Be a team player.
   B. Support churchwide emphases and events.
5. If possible, share the first draft of the calendar with broader groups in the youth ministry family. Teenagers, parents, and leaders may see conflicts or other potential problems the planning team missed.
6. The completed youth ministry calendar is an important communication and promotion tool. It should be distributed widely.
7. Send the yearlong calendar to all adult leaders.
8. Send all key summer dates to parents as soon as the annual calendar is completed.
9. Send calendars to parents and youth on a monthly basis, in order to include more details.

The Youth Minister's Role in Planning

Although the best planning for youth ministry is a team effort, the minister of youth is the central person in that process. That person's calling, character, and competence will shape much of the church's work with youth.

Every congregation with teenagers should have a youth minister or someone performing the role of a youth minister. A variety of people might fill that role.

In some churches the pastor may fill this position. In addition to his churchwide ministry, he also may tie together all that the church is doing with and for youth, youth workers, and parents of youth.

In other churches a staff member may have other staff assignments in addition to serving as a youth ministry coordinator. Possible titles include minister of music and youth, minister of education and youth, and other combinations.

In still other churches a committed volunteer serves as youth ministry coordinator. He or she gives full attention to orchestrating the church's various programs and ministries with youth, youth workers, and parents of youth. In some churches a married couple may share the position.

Paid leaders often have the title minister of youth, youth pastor, student pastor, student minister, associate pastor with youth, or one of the combination titles above. Some volunteers also have the title minister of youth. They perceive themselves as members of the church's ministerial staff.

Other volunteers feel more comfortable with titles such as youth ministry coordinator, youth director, or youth chairperson. They realize they occupy a vital church leadership position, but they do not see themselves as members of the pastoral staff. The title youth ministry coordinator is growing in popularity and is most descriptive of this position.

THE NEED FOR A LEADER

There are many reasons why every church with teenagers needs a youth minister or volunteer youth ministry coordinator.
   1. Every youth ministry needs someone who sees the big picture.
   2. Every youth ministry needs someone to build motivation and excitement.
   3. Every youth ministry needs someone to communicate purpose and vision.

4. Every youth ministry needs someone to chair and guide a core planning team.
5. Every youth ministry needs someone to plan and administer the youth budget.
6. Every youth ministry needs someone to give visibility to the church's work with youth.
7. Every youth ministry needs someone to coordinate and balance the work of the weekly youth ministries and organizations.
8. Every youth ministry needs someone to take the lead in enlisting and training other adults to serve with youth.

Lead Teams

Most youth ministers spend most of their time managing events. That is an unfortunate fact of life. Preparing for "the next big thing" consumes the majority of most youth ministers' hours. That may have been all right in an earlier era, but it may not be adequate for ministry today. Too much time in event management means too little time:

- Sharing one's faith with an increasing percentage of lost teenagers
- Intervening and counseling with troubled teenagers
- Coordinating several education organizations for teenagers
- Coordinating programming and personal ministry for parents
- Guiding the church in setting a direction for youth ministry and in calendar planning
- Coordinating a ministry to school campuses
- Enlisting, training, and motivating a growing group of adult leaders
- And dozens of "other duties as assigned"

Intensifying the issue is the fact that the vast majority of youth ministers are volunteer, part-time, or in combination roles. This means all the above duties must be accomplished without even the benefit of a full workweek. Too many hours of event busywork can be critical. There has to be a better way.

An alternative method of planning is to organize teams of youth, adult leaders, and parents who will give leadership to major programming elements. Lead teams should not be confused with groups or committees who "help the youth minister" with an event. What is unique about lead teams is that they take ultimate responsibility for an event. Lead teams don't help the youth minister; the youth minister helps teams who are fully committed to seeing events through. Lead teams are a prime example of ministry teams that flow out of and into corporate worship, open groups, and closed groups.

Key Concepts

1. Lead teams are assembled to accomplish a particular task or mission and exist only long enough to fulfill that objective.
2. Lead teams accept ultimate responsibility for their chosen event, project, or campaign. The pastoral leadership team of their church serves to motivate, inspire, and give direction to their work, but the team has ultimate responsibility for their event or ministry.
3. Lead teams do not implement the dreams of a core planning team. The core planning team assists lead teams in making their dreams become reality.
4. Lead teams serve to implement events, projects, or campaigns according to a design and spirit consistent with the overall vision and direction of the entire congregation.
5. Lead teams do not do all the work on projects. They may involve many members in their work. They simply take the lead, coordinating role.

Administration

The Purposes of Lead Teams
1. To assist youth ministers in moving to a leadership style that emphasizes equipping church members to do the work of ministry in the spirit of Ephesians 4:11-12.
2. To enable youth ministers to shift time from event and project management to roles in ministry more unique to their calling and gifts.
3. To enable youth ministers to better balance their total work hours and weekly schedules.
4. To open opportunities for lay leaders to fully express their calling and giftedness in ministry.

Lead Team Structure
Lead teams are composed of youth, adult leaders, and parents. Both generations bring strengths to the process. Each church determines the number of team members needed. Here are two examples:

Larger Church Lead Team

1. High school youth	1. Seasoned youth leader—chairperson
2. High school youth	2. Youth leader
3. Junior high youth	3. Parent
4. Junior high youth	4. Parent

Smaller Church Lead Team

1. High school youth	1. Seasoned youth leader—chairperson
2. Junior high youth	2. Parent

Meeting Times and Places
Most churches will experience greater success when active lead teams meet simultaneously to plan. There are several advantages:
1. The youth minister can spend the entire time going team to team, offering encouragement, solving problems, and ensuring the quality of plans underway.
2. When teams meet at the same time, attendance is more visible and team members feel more accountable to attend.
3. Members feel more excitement seeing a larger number of team members at work.
4. Potential schedule or resource conflicts between teams can be solved quickly and easily.

If possible, meeting times should be tied to other weekly church events. Ministers need to protect a prime meeting time for lead teams each month, without conflicts. Monthly, simultaneous meetings will be about right for most churches. Teams quickly approaching their event may decide to plan additional meetings or work sessions.

A team chairperson and the youth minister should decide how many months before an event a team should begin meeting. Complicated projects such as an out-of-state mission trip may require a six-month head start. A simple activity at the church may only require two months.

Chairpersons
The youth minister handpicks the chairperson of every team. That selection cannot be left to chance. The selection of the chairperson may be the most important variable in the effectiveness of lead team ministry. Chairpersons must be seasoned youth leaders who

sidering the lead team concept may honestly wonder, *How do I know that teams actually will do quality work? How can I monitor them while they are in the planning stages?*

There are no guarantees that teams will do quality work. Teams in scores of churches across the nation are indeed providing first-class events, activities, and projects. Most don't want to be associated with leading a flop. Much more importantly, most want to maximize their impact for the kingdom.

Youth ministers can monitor the quality of planning in at least three ways. First, they can move from team to team during the regularly scheduled team meeting sessions. Visiting informally with a team provides some sense of how they are progressing in their plans. No team wants a third-degree grilling, but light questions are not offensive and provide the feedback the youth minister needs.

Second, youth ministers can request a copy of each team's minutes at the end of meeting times. If the church has a copy machine, it is much easier to get minutes copied as the teams are dismissing than sometime later in the week. Team minutes provide very important feedback concerning both the quality and the direction of the team's planning.

Third, youth ministers should stay in touch with chairpersons informally between scheduled team meetings. Church hallway conversations, phone calls, and even lunches together provide valuable feedback. Once again, no one enjoys an FBI-styled questioning. Instead, youth ministers should initiate conversations with questions such as, "Jim, is there any information I need to get you about your retreat? Any help you need from the ministers?" Gentle questions in the context of offering help and showing interest generally lead to the feedback the youth minister needs.

THE YOUTH MINISTER'S INVOLVEMENT

The previous paragraphs infer that the youth minister (or volunteer coordinator) must stay involved with lead teams if this approach is to be effective. That is an absolute fact. Youth ministers who start lead teams and then assume they will work without his or her involvement are headed for a crisis. Teams abandoned by the youth minister lose focus. They hit problems they don't know how to solve. They get behind. They feel negative toward the youth minister. It is not a pretty picture.

A youth minister might sincerely say, "I am excited about starting lead teams because their work will allow me to start or expand some things I have always wanted to be doing. But if I have to stay involved with all these teams for this thing to work, what advantage is there?" Here is the answer. It is possible to give the teams the support and direction they need in a fraction of the time it takes to do the event yourself. A youth minister might spend 20 hours doing all the work on a high school mission trip, but only 2 hours guiding a mission trip lead team. The other 18 hours can be given to brand-new ministries, or even an occasional evening at home.

Affirmation

Youth ministers must creatively plan how genuinely to affirm the work of lead team members. The lead team strategy will crumble without it. To the degree possible, team members need to be in spotlighted roles at the event on which they have spent months working. The youth minister (or volunteer coordinator) needs to give groups and audiences creative ways to affirm their work. Affirmation from the pulpit immediately after an event is important, too. Genuine affirmation is both Christian and a key to future motivation for lead team service.

> **And He personally gave some to be apostles, some prophets, some evangelists, some pastors and teachers, for the training of the saints in the work of ministry, to build up the body of Christ (Eph. 4:11-12).**

How to Sell the Strategy

Selling the church on the lead team strategy is a three-step process.

1. Present the strategy to the pastor. Make an appointment that will allow time for you to make a complete presentation. Emphasize each of the points discussed below, especially how this plan will allow you to expand your own ministry in new areas. If he is generally supportive, then move ahead with the next steps.
2. Present the strategy to a few key youth ministry volunteers. Choose one to three leaders whose opinions are respected by others, and who are close enough to you to give honest feedback. These are folk who likely will chair key lead teams if the strategy is accepted. If they are ready to move forward with you, move to the next step.
3. Present the plan to all youth, parents, and workers. You might call this a Town Hall Meeting to communicate it is not just another church meeting. A strong attendance is absolutely essential. In fact, the lead team strategy will not work unless a fair percentage of the youth ministry family buys into the concept at the very beginning. Consequently, you pull out all the stops for this one meeting. You make personal calls and home visits. You include food if appropriate. You commit people to bring things. You enlist youth workers who will ensure the attendance of their class members. You let parents know decisions will be made at this meeting that will vitally affect their teenage children from now until graduation. You enlist pulpit support from the pastor. You don't leave anything to chance. Your presentation at the Town Hall Meeting will be one of the more important talks you will give in a church. That presentation deserves several hours of preparation and prayer. Much is at stake. Here is a possible outline:

   A. "The Bible suggests a better way for us to organize our youth ministry." Lead the group in a word by word study of Ephesians 4:11-12. Compare the reading of the *King James Version* (which is easy to misunderstand) and newer translations. Emphasize that ministers are given gifts primarily to be used in equipping the saints so that the saints can perform the work of the ministry. Use commentaries and Bible study tools to prepare a thorough study.

   Confess that too often you have asked others to help you do the work of the ministry, rather than equipping them for their own calling and ministry. Explain there may be a way to organize youth ministry closer to the New Testament pattern.

   B. "There may be a better way to organize our youth ministry that would allow us to expand and move into any areas where we sense God at work." Explain that with the present organization, it is difficult to add new ministries. You may even want to say that because you are basically in charge of everything, you simply don't have time to consider adding new programs or ministries.

   Present the possibility that there may be a way to organize that would allow the church to respond quickly to new needs and opportunities that emerge, and to begin new ministries in response to seeing God at work.

   C. "There may be a plan that would allow me as a minister (or the volunteer youth ministry coordinator) to move into new areas of ministry." This part of the address would be unique to you, but you might say things similar to:
   - "I have always wished I could offer a counseling ministry with troubled youth and parents. The way we are organized now, I am only able to give them a quick pat on the head. The needs are great."
   - "I so wish I could spend time on our school campuses. It takes time to get to lunches and activities at seven different schools, but I feel I have a witness that

is needed there. The way we are organized now, that simply isn't possible."
- "I have always wanted to start a new drama ministry in our church. Drama can be a great evangelism and discipleship tool, but at present there are no minutes available for that ministry."

D. "Hundreds of churches are adopting a strategy that is New Testament in design, allows them to move into many new areas of youth ministry, and allows their youth ministers to utilize fully their gifts and calling in ministry." At this point, present the lead team strategy. Adapt the strategy to fit your church's situation. Use handouts and visuals to aid communication. Allow open discussion and provide positive answers to questions that may arise.

If the youth ministry family seems open to the strategy, enthusiastically announce the date the group will reassemble to choose teams. Ideally, this meeting should be exactly one week away.

It may not be best to organize teams at the original Town Hall Meeting. First, the youth minister needs time to enlist chairpersons after the strategy is adopted. Also, if the youth minister begins putting up team posters at the end of the Town Hall Meeting, he or she in essence is saying, "I knew you people would go for my plan." It just seems better to delay the organizational meeting a week or two.

Administering the Youth Ministry Budget

For the strongest budget proposal possible, present the figures as the anticipated costs of funding a strategic plan built on the five functions of the church and on your priorities and goals. Budget planning committees have been trained from birth to cut the budget proposals submitted by ministers. The youth minister who just turns in a "lump sum" request is almost certain to have it axed. Submitting a clear, strategic plan changes everything. Whereas cutting a lump sum is painless, cutting out specific ministry events tied to vital priorities and goals isn't. The more thorough and well-thought-out the plan, the better the odds it will be adopted.

SAMPLE LINE ITEMS
(These are the lines that typically appear in budget reports to the church.)
  I. Ongoing Youth Ministry (Weekly organizations, ongoing ministries, supplies)
 II. Youth Ministry In-Town Events (DiscipleNow, lock-ins, parent events, etc.)
III. Youth Ministry Major Trips (See below.)
IV. Lead Teams (See below.)

Sample Detail Under Line Items:
(This is detail that goes to the budget planning committee.)
  I. Ongoing Youth Ministry
 II. Youth Ministry In-Town Events
III. Youth Ministry Major Trips

    A. Youth Camp . . . . $ _____
         Sponsor Fees . . . . $ _____
         Bus Rentals . . . . $ _____
         Road Meals . . . . $ _____
         Scholarships . . . . $ _____
         Honoraria . . . . $ _____
         Study Materials . . . . $ _____
         Rec. Equipment . . . . $ _____
    B. Winter Ski Trip (Similar Detail) . . . . $ _____
    C. Spring Retreat (Similar Detail) . . . . $ _____

Each lead team chairperson needs clear guidance on the money his or her team has available to spend. The easiest way to communicate this is with a budget line item for "Lead Team Events." Chairpersons quickly can see the amounts they have to spend. Since budget reports are public, chairpersons tend to take those limits seriously.

IV. Lead Team Events
         New Year's Eve Lock-in . . . . $ _____
         Youth Week . . . . $ _____
         Spring Retreat . . . . $ _____
         Summer Splash . . . . $ _____
         DiscipleNow Weekend . . . . $ _____

MOVE EXPENSES WHERE THEY BELONG

Placing all the church is investing in youth ministry in only one line item can be confusing to church members and may result in budget reductions. When youth ministry funds are listed in one line item only, often that figure will be hundreds or thousands of dollars more than the figure for other age-group ministries. In reality, the nature of youth ministry necessitates more expense. At the same time, there is no need to make one very large figure serve as a lightning rod for criticism. Here are reasonable alternatives:

A. If appropriate, place funds for study books and curricula in line items associated with the educational ministries of the church.

B. If appropriate, place funds for teacher training in line items associated with the educational ministries of the church.

C. If appropriate, place funds for parent ministry in line items associated with adult ministries or family ministries of the church.

D. If appropriate, place funds for league fees and sports equipment in a church recreation line item.

E. If appropriate, place funds for a youth mission trip under a "Missions" line item.

F. If appropriate, place funds for a youth choir trip under the music ministry line item.

LEADING THE CHURCH TO INCREASE THE YOUTH BUDGET

1. If it strengthens your case for a rather dramatic increase in the youth ministry budget, print out the percent of the total church budget that youth ministry has represented over the past few years. In many cases, increases in youth ministry funds have not kept pace with the increases in the total budget.

2. If it strengthens your case for a rather dramatic increase in the youth ministry budget, print out the amount the church has invested per active youth over the past

Administration

few years. It may be that the youth ministry budget has not increased commensurate with the growth in active youth.

WHAT TO EXPECT OF FAMILIES WITH YOUTH
Ask yourself, *If these students were not involved in a church youth ministry, what would they be spending anyway?*
   A. What would those students spend on school or team trips?
   B. What would those students do with their friends for recreation or social life?
   C. What T-shirts, books, or other items would they buy for other organizations?

Seek to keep what families spend through the youth ministry of your church comparable to what other families are spending in the community.

Building a Prayer Strategy for Youth Ministry

An amazing number of youth leaders give careful attention to transportation, sponsors, food, and many other event details—but never call youth and adults to cover events with prayer. Yet those same leaders know the salvation and spiritual transformation of youth flows from prayer—not meticulous planning. The following are just some of the ways teenagers and adults can be mobilized to intercede over every element of youth ministry.

PRAYER BRACELETS
- Names of all youth and leaders to be involved in some project are placed on bracelets.
- Names of lost youth can be used—with initials to protect privacy.
- Provide a printed prayer guide so intercessors will know specifically how to pray.
- Allow those who prayed to meet those for whom they prayed.
- Bracelets are available from hospital supply houses.

24-HOUR PRAYER VIGILS
- Consider 30-minute segments intercessors will fill.
- Be realistic in how much time to try and fill—lots of blank spots are discouraging.
- Provide a printed prayer guide to direct the prayers of intercessors.
- Ensure teenagers understand the prayer covering they are receiving.
- Consider inviting intercessors to pray at home if nights at church are not options.

PRAYER ROOMS DURING EVENTS
- Consider adding a rug, kneeling rail, indirect lighting, and visual focal point (cross or portrait).
- Provide soft, instrumental worship music.
- Provide a Bible, printed prayer guides, and prayer requests.
- If practical, invite those attending the event to go to the prayer room to be prayed over.
- If practical, place cards in the chairs at the event for those who want to send requests to the prayer room.
- Consider forwarding written prayer requests to the youth minister for prayer and follow-up after the event.
- If practical, mail a note to those requesting prayer, letting them know they were prayed for.

YOUTH MINISTRY PRAYER ROOM YEAR-ROUND
- Create a physical setting similar to the description above.
- Provide an ongoing way for prayer requests to get to the room.
- Invite youth, adult leaders, and parents to pray as they will, or enlist intercessors to come on a schedule.

PRAYER WALKING
- Prayer walk event facilities you will use.
- Prayer walk neighborhoods you seek to reach.
- Prayer walk school hallways, government buildings, or other focal points for ministry.
- Prayer walk places of vice and spiritual strongholds.

The Youth Minister's Role with the Adult Leadership Team

The youth minister is a minister to the adults who work with youth. Those adults are part of his or her flock. The youth minister is called to spend a portion of every week equipping them for the work of youth ministry. The youth minister is called to be the visionary leader who calls out the very best in adults—in the context of a warm relationship with each of them. Here are principles that flesh out that ministry.

Principle: You are a minister before you are a youth minister.
Application: Respond to adult leaders with such needs as hospitalization, death of close relatives, birth of a child, and other needs.
Principle: Adults are more willing to work at implementing their plans.
Application: Work through teams that allow leaders to birth new directions for ministry.
Principle: Most adult leaders desire a close relationship with the youth minister.
Application: Try to spend a few minutes in personal conversation with every adult leader every time the leader is present.
Principle: Vocational ministers are equippers.
Application: Work toward the day each adult leader will say, "Once I simply served to make my youth minister successful. Now my youth minister simply serves to make me successful in the ministry God has given me."
Principle: Adult leaders strongly dislike failing at what they do.
Application: Train each adult leader with the skills he or she needs before placing him or her in a leadership role.
Principle: Adults tend to remain on spiritual plateaus.
Application: Create times and places to impact the spiritual growth of adults as powerful as those targeted to youth.
Principle: Adults tend to fulfill the expectations—either low or high—youth ministers have of them.
Application: Work in concert with the leadership team to develop a covenant of expectations that each will commit to.
Principle: The ability to relate effectively to youth can be a learned behavior.
Application: Teach adult leaders everything you know about how to create and sustain ministry-quality relationships with teenagers.
Principle: Adults are more willing to give effort when their work is acknowledged.
Application: Keep the spotlight on organizations and ministries headed by adult leaders—through publicity, budget, schedules, and your personal support.

Principle: Adults work more effectively when they feel close to other adult leaders.
Application: Create fellowship and prayer experiences for the adult team with the same excellence as those for youth.
Principle: Adults experience daily minor and major frustrations.
Application: Creatively find ways to reduce frustrations for adults in their leadership roles. Consistently take actions that support them and make their work less stressful.
Principle: Volunteers in an enterprise feel more valued when they receive early or more extensive information than the rank-and-file.
Application: Communicate full information about youth ministry plans to adult leaders before making announcements to the youth group.
Principle: Volunteers in an enterprise feel more valued when their opinions are solicited early in the planning process.
Application: Ask for reflections and feedback from core adult leaders before making any major change in youth ministry.
Principle: When the youth minister trains adult leaders, he or she should model the same high quality expected of leaders.
Application: Don't lecture while teaching teachers not to lecture. Use a variety of educational methods diverse enough to cover all styles of learning.
Principle: Adults are significantly blessed and motivated by leading youth to Christ.
Application: Create opportunities for adults to share Christ with students at every ministry event that is practical.
Principle: Many toxic adults (but not all) won't wait for delayed access to youth.
Application: Require a six-month waiting period before new members can have direct contact with youth.
Principle: Most adults convicted of crimes against youth repeat those crimes again.
Application: Perform background checks on every adult who will have direct access with youth, with no exceptions. Adults with nothing to hide and who truly care for youth will welcome this action.
Principle: Adults are more effective when they work in partnership with parents.
Application: Plan at least an annual opportunity for adult leaders to meet informally with parents.
Principle: Where there is no vision, the people perish.
Application: Choose to be a dynamic leader every time you are before the adult leaders. Keep the mission statement before them. Continually help them see your vision for the future.

Adult Leaders and Youth Behavior

You must both train and empower your leadership team to implement official discipline guidelines. Times of teaching and worship are primary in church life. Teenagers and other members who come to church in order to learn and grow deserve to study and worship in an atmosphere where that is possible without hindrance. Leaders have a responsibility to maintain that atmosphere.

Teenagers who make study or worship impossible for those around them need to be moved to an alternative study location. Generally, this will mean spending the remainder of the time with the youth minister or other youth leader. Before dismissing a youth from a class or service, leaders have a responsibility to tell a youth his or her behavior warrants dismissal. Youth who choose to continue disrupting should be dismissed. In most cases, leaders should inform parents when a dismissal has taken place. This is especially true for junior high students. In most cases, a youth who has been dismissed from a group should be welcome at the next meeting.

Youth who choose to participate in youth activities agree to follow the instructions of leaders. Obeying those instructions and exhibiting respect toward leaders should be a condition for remaining at an activity. At the same time, leaders need to try and discover what is motivating a youth to misbehave. The youth ministry family should seek to meet those needs if possible. See the "Discipline" section in the "Fellowship" chapter for more suggestions on working with problem teenagers.

Coordinating Parent Ministry

The youth minister is a minister to parents of youth. As with adult leaders, parents of youth are part of his or her flock. The youth minister is called to spend part of every week in ministry to parents and in creating programming that will impact them and their families.

Every youth minister needs a vision for dramatically expanded impact on families. Here are dreams that have guided this author's work across three decades of local-church youth ministry:

1. I have a dream that Christian parents will again turn their hearts toward their children, including their teenage children. (Mal. 4:6; Luke 1:17)
2. I have a dream that Christian teenagers—because of new warmth and intimacy flowing from their parents—will turn their hearts toward those parents.
3. I have a dream that parents will be the most important disciplers and Bible teachers of their children.
4. I have a dream that parents and teenagers will experience intimate and vibrant worship as families.
5. I have a dream that parents and teenagers will experience joyful recreation and fellowship as families.
6. I have a dream that parents and teenagers will bring under their roofs and influence spiritually lost teenagers.
7. I have a dream that parents and teenagers will bring under their roofs and influence teenage believers whose parents are spiritually lost—and thus need mentoring, discipling, and the modeling of Christian home life.
8. I have a dream that parents will begin saving at the birth of a child to fund that child's going to the front lines of missions during high school or college.
9. I have a dream that families will perform acts of ministry and service together, both locally and internationally.
10. I have a dream that teenagers empowered through heart connections with their parents will—in God's sovereign timing—lead the church into revival and culture into a spiritual awakening.
11. I have a dream that parents will champion their teenagers following God's clear call, even if that call should entail sacrifice, risk, or even martyrdom.

Parent Meetings or Seminars

Perhaps the most visible expression of an expanded ministry with parents will be regular meetings or seminars for that group. Volunteer and bivocational youth ministers should consider planning at least two parent meetings each year. Fully-funded youth ministers should consider planning more of such events. This may represent a stretch for both groups, but the impact on families and the kingdom will be worth it.

Hitting on perceived needs is the key to attendance and involvement. Here are several topics most parents would find interesting:

- Making a Spiritual Impact on Your Teenager
- How to Communicate with Your Teenager
- How to Discipline Your Teen
- The Impact of the Health of Your Marriage on Your Teenager
- Practical Ways Parents Can Support and Strengthen Our Church's Youth Ministry
- A Vision for Seeing Your Teenager Spend a Summer or Longer in Missions While Young
- When True Love Doesn't Wait
- What Are Normal and What Are Dangerous Signs in Your Teenager's Behavior?
- Alcohol and Other Drugs
- Understanding Postmodern Students
- Teens and Media
- Living as a Blended Family
- Transitions to Middle School, High School, and College
- Family Financial Management
- Helping Teenagers Understand Death and Dying
- Preparing Your Child and Your Pocketbook for College
- Bringing Your Family Schedule Under Control
- The Dark Side of the Online World
- Responding to Bullies and Bullying

Other youth ministry programming possibilities include:

- Intensive Parenting Courses
- Parent and Youth Dialogue Events
- Parent and Youth Retreats
- Parent and Youth Banquets
- Parent and Youth Social Events
- Parent and Youth Mission Projects

Conclusion

Putting the different pieces of youth ministry together is like working on a complex puzzle. It helps to see the big picture. First, some of the keys to success include involving as many adults and teenagers in the administration and leadership process as possible. As mentioned, lead teams are an excellent way to do this. Second, plan on frequent and as comprehensive evaluation times as possible. Develop an evaluation instrument based on the five functions of the church in the area of youth ministry and examine how you are doing. Third, bathe the entire process in prayer, before, during, and after planning periods. Allow God to be the driving force in what you are doing and you won't be able to prevent your church from establishing a successful youth ministry.

---

[1] Doug Fields, *Purpose-Driven Youth Ministry,* Grand Rapids: Zondervan, 2000, 44.
[2] George Barna, *The Power of Vision,* Ventura: Gospel Light Publications, 2003.
[3] Willow Creek Community Church, *Church Leaders Handbook,* p. 173.
[4] Rick Warren, *The Purpose-Driven Church,* Grand Rapids: Zondervan, 1999, 112.
[5] Doug Fields, *Purpose-Driven Youth Ministry,* Grand Rapids: Zondervan, 2000, 88-91.

Appendix 1

FAITH

Ask: What do you understand it takes for a person to go to heaven?
Say: Consider how the Bible answers this question. It is a matter of FAITH.

When presenting the gospel to youth, use these truths and their Scriptures.

F is for FORGIVENESS
We cannot have eternal life and heaven without God's forgiveness.—Read Ephesians 1:7a.

A is for AVAILABLE
Forgiveness is available. It is—
- Available for all.—Read John 3:16.
- But not automatic.—Read Matthew 7:21a.

I is for IMPOSSIBLE
It is impossible for God to allow sin into heaven.
- Because of who He is: God is loving and just. His judgment is against sin.—Read James 2:13a.
- Because of who we are: Every person is a sinner.—Read Romans 3:23.

But how can a sinful person enter heaven when God allows no sin?

T is for TURN
Turn means repent.
- Turn from something—sin and self.—Read Luke 13:3b.
- Turn to Someone; trust Christ only.—Read Romans 10:9.

H is for HEAVEN
Heaven is eternal life.
- Here—Read John 10:10b.
- Hereafter—Read John 14:3.
- How?

How can a person have God's forgiveness, heaven and eternal life, and Jesus as personal Savior and Lord?
By trusting in Christ and asking Him for forgiveness. Take the step of faith described by another meaning of FAITH: Forsaking All I Trust Him.

Use this sample prayer in the next paragraph when leading a teenager to receive Christ as Savior. Pray the prayer aloud, one phrase at a time, allowing the teenager to repeat the phrase after you. Then, conclude the prayer by personally thanking God for the youth's decision to become a believer.

Prayer: Lord Jesus, I know I am a sinner and have displeased You in many ways. I believe You died for my sin and only through faith in Your death and resurrection can I be forgiven. I want to turn from my sin and ask You to come into my life as my Savior and Lord. From this day on, I will follow You by living a life that pleases You. Thank You, Lord Jesus, for saving me. Amen.

Explain that accepting Christ is the beginning. Urge the youth to follow Christ in baptism and to unite with a church. Encourage the youth to be faithful in Sunday School, worship at church, and a daily personal worship experience with God.

Through love and prayer, you can lead youth to Christ.

Appendix 2

Checklist for Evaluating Bible Study Resources

I. Content
- [ ] 1. Is the Bible the main source for the content?
- [ ] 2. Is the Bible treated authoritatively as the inspired Word of God?
- [ ] 3. Is the biblical commentary on the events and teachings of Scripture portrayed accurately, as opposed to interpretations that may be potentially negative?
- [ ] 4. Are the Scripture translations used accurate and reliable, or are they paraphrases?
- [ ] 5. Do the materials emphasize distinctly Christian values?
- [ ] 6. Are students encouraged to examine their own values in light of the biblical content?
- [ ] 7. Does the content encourage students to make a personal commitment to Jesus Christ?
- [ ] 8. Are Christian students assisted in developing their faith and trust in God?
- [ ] 9. Are critical life issues addressed?
- [ ] 10. Are current life situations portrayed realistically?
- [ ] 11. Is there a connection made between the student's relationship with God and his or her relationship with others?
- [ ] 12. Is the content age-appropriate?
- [ ] 13. Are age-appropriate methodologies utilized?
- [ ] 14. Do the materials appeal to the cultural experiences and interests of the students?
- [ ] 15. Is there a plan to involve students in a systematic study of the entire Word of God?
- [ ] 16. Are home and family situations adequately and accurately addressed?

II. Appearance and Organization
- [ ] 1. Is the layout appealing to youth?
- [ ] 2. Is there an interesting use of color?
- [ ] 3. Are the pictures and artwork contemporary and appealing?
- [ ] 4. Are the materials appropriately designed for student abilities, needs, and interests?

III. Teaching Considerations
- [ ] 1. Are the materials easy to use by inexperienced teachers?
- [ ] 2. Are the teaching materials helpful?
- [ ] 3. Are suggestions given for helping the teacher plan?
- [ ] 4. Are suggestions given to help the teacher evaluate the learning experience?
- [ ] 5. Are teaching objectives and goals clearly stated?
- [ ] 6. Does the content focus on the stated goals and main ideas?
- [ ] 7. Are suggestions given for additional study resources for the teacher?
- [ ] 8. Are teaching aids provided or suggested?
- [ ] 9. Is the material easily adaptable for varying groups of students?
- [ ] 10. Is the teacher encouraged to use a variety of teaching methods?
- [ ] 11. Is the material teacher-centered or does it allow for maximum student involvement?
- [ ] 12. Is consideration given to various levels of student abilities?
- [ ] 13. Do the teaching plans make wise use of time?

IV. Learning Considerations
- [ ] 1. Are students challenged to make life responses, as opposed to just understanding facts?
- [ ] 2. Are students assisted in knowing how to apply biblical principles?
- [ ] 3. Are application and interpretation both emphasized?
- [ ] 4. Are students engaged intellectually and emotionally, as well as spiritually?
- [ ] 5. Are students encouraged to think and respond freely?
- [ ] 6. Are students' various learning styles considered?
- [ ] 7. Are opportunities given for students to participate in cooperative learning?

Appendix 3

Safety and Legal Issues

In Chapter 3, the issues of safety and legal liability were surfaced, but a little more attention is warranted. It would be impossible to fully address all of the issues of personal safety and property security fellowships might reveal in a forum like this, but here are a few things to consider:

1. Form a response plan for dealing with emergencies and make sure your leaders are aware of it. Keep a well-stocked first-aid kit available and insist on having at least one individual who is first-aid and CPR trained at your events. Being prepared consistently is the number one safety priority.

2. Thoroughly prepare recreation areas to remove any foreseeable hazard before you begin.

3. Insist on written parental permission when taking students on trips away from the local area or overnight. Also, be sure to secure medical release forms when taking students on trips.

4. Set down specific written policies and guidelines for vehicle operation. Address who may operate vehicles during a youth group function and how they are to operate the vehicles. Also, screen your drivers. Anyone with a poor driving record should be excluded from operating a vehicle on your behalf, and never let a student drive as a part of an event!

5. When in doubt err on the side of being conservative. When youth are in your care, you are held to a legal standard of "responsible care." Your responsibility can be explained using the Latin term *In loco parentis,* which means "in the place of parents." When you agree to take responsibility for a teenager, you also agree to safeguard him or her responsibly from harm.

6. Establish policies for recruiting, training, and supervising workers.

7. Review your insurance coverage to determine if there are specific programming actions you are prohibited from conducting. Some insurance carriers go so far as to exclude certain recreation activities by name such as the infamous game, "Chubby Bunny." Strange but true!

Appendix 4

*Adopted at the Southern Baptist Youth Ministry Summit
February 2, 2003.*

Mission Statement

As denominational leaders in Southern Baptist student ministry, we desire to serve the local churches as they accomplish the Great Commission in and through the lives of youth and their families.

We Value Southern Baptist Student Ministry That Advances the kingdom of God and that ...

- Is Bible-centered
- Is driven by prayer
- Is empowered by the Holy Spirit
- Seeks spiritual transformation through evangelism and discipleship
- Is church-based
- Is mission-focused
- Is family supportive
- Is relational
- Involves adults using their gifts
- Encourages youth in leadership

Foundations of Southern Baptist Student Ministry Strategy

- We believe the mission of student ministry is the accomplishment of the Great Commission and obedience to the Great Commandment.
- We believe the purposes of student ministry are evangelism, discipleship, ministry, fellowship, and worship under the guidance of the Holy Spirit.
- We believe that numerical growth, lifelong spiritual growth and transformation, ministry expansion, and kingdom advancement often are indications of student ministry performance of the five purposes.
- We believe in winning, discipling, and equipping parents to be primary spiritual leaders for their children.
- We believe in providing open groups for all youth that focus on foundational evangelism and discipleship.
- We believe in providing opportunities for youth who desire deeper discipleship content, lifestyle and attendance accountability, and study and spiritual preparation between meetings.
- We believe in equipping students and their leaders to make a clear and relevant presentation of the gospel.
- We believe in biblical baptism for all converts.
- We believe in local church membership.
- We believe in calling students, parents, and leaders to an ongoing prayer strategy to undergird student ministry.
- We believe in involving youth in multiple avenues of worship during which they experience God, including the full congregation, families, youth settings, and personal worship.
- We believe in training youth to use music and fine arts as tools of worship, evangelism, and discipleship.
- We believe every student ministry event, organization, and ministry must have clearly defined target audiences and must be designed to accomplish one or more of the student ministry purposes.
- We believe in training, mobilizing, and sending youth and their leaders to meet spiritual and physical needs of all people in the name of Jesus both locally and globally.
- We believe in educating and training youth to create and implement strategies to evangelize and minister to target cultures, both locally and globally.
- We believe in providing consistent encouragement and guidance to youth sensing a call of God to Christian ministry vocations.
- We believe in challenging every student to spend a summer or longer in full-time missions service during high school or college.
- We believe in equipping youth to fulfill the ministries to which they have been called, including ministry roles they are to fill now in student ministry, in the congregation, and in the broader Kingdom.
- We believe in calling out adults who sense they are called by God to minister with youth, and to disciple and equip those adults for their ministries.
- We believe student ministry belongs to the congregation under the leadership of the Holy Spirit rather than to an individual.
- We believe that representative youth, leaders, and parents should be mobilized to establish a student ministry's purpose and vision; choose priorities; select organizations, events, and ministries; and implement youth ministry plans in accordance with the church's mission statement.
- We believe student ministry must bond ethnically and socially diverse youth into a uniquely Christian subculture characterized by biblical community and joyful fellowship.
- We believe in equipping youth, parents, and leaders to represent the Great Physician in the lives of hurting youth and families.
- We believe that obedience to God results in a lifestyle that is holy and pure for youth, youth leaders, and parents.
- We believe student ministry assists people in moving into and beyond the teenage years.

Appendix 5

Minister of Youth Job Description (Sample)

This is a sample job description. The language and format need to be customized to a particular situation.

The minister of youth is called by God to follow Christ in a life of discipleship, utilizing the leadership gifts given by the Holy Spirit to lead the church in carrying out the Great Commission for the purpose of expanding the kingdom of God.

THE MINISTER OF YOUTH WILL—

1. Minister
- Serve as an integral member of the pastoral ministry team, and give full support to the leadership role of the senior pastor.
- Provide pastoral ministry with the youth ministry family (youth, parents of youth, and youth leaders), and coordinate the training of others to do likewise.

2. Administer
- Coordinate the weekly youth education organizations. In cooperation with the minister of education, coordinate an overall youth curriculum plan for the church, leading to properly sequenced, balanced, and comprehensive Christian education for youth active in the youth organizations for six years.
- Coordinate the creation of the annual youth ministry budget proposal, and administer that budget as approved by the budget planning committee.
- Coordinate programming and events for parents of youth related to their parenting roles, and events for parents and youth.
- Coordinate space utilization in youth ministry and make recommendations concerning building and remodeling needs.
- Assist the youth organizations in providing opportunities for members of the youth ministry family to be directly involved in missions and ministry, both locally and away.
- Coordinate the training and mentoring of members of the youth ministry family sensing a call to ministry vocations.
- Coordinate planning to ensure Christian youth experience authentic worship personally, with the youth group, and with the full church body.
- Coordinate planning to ensure youth experience true fellowship within the body of Christ.

3. Lead
- Guide the youth ministry family to define, communicate, and implement its purpose and strategy.
- Represent youth ministry on the church leadership team and with other church groups as called on.
- Chair the core planning team, guide the development of the youth ministry calendar, and coordinate youth ministry lead teams.
- Coordinate the enlisting, discipling, training, and motivating of adults to serve in youth ministry, in cooperation with the nominating committee.
- Fine-tune skills in leading, administering, ministering and communicating through a structured reading plan, high quality conferences, and formal education.

4. Communicate
- Share the gospel with lost youth and lost parents on an ongoing basis, both individually and corporately.
- Coordinate an overall youth evangelism strategy for the church, ensure evangelism is a goal of all youth programming, and coordinate continuing training in soul winning for all members of the youth ministry family.
- Network with other evangelical youth leaders in the community to support youth in starting and strengthening school campus ministries, and to coordinate events designed to evangelize and disciple youth.
- Coordinate the training of youth to serve as missionaries to their school campuses.
- As allowed by law, minister on the secondary school campuses within the sphere of influence of the church.
- Coordinate youth ministry communication and promotion plans in concert with lead teams, youth organizations, and pastoral ministers.

ACCOUNTABILITY
The minister of youth reports to the minister of education (or pastor), and supervises interns and volunteer youth staff.

CHRISTIAN GROWTH STUDY PLAN
Preparing Christians to Serve

In the Christian Growth Study Plan (formerly Church Study Course), this book *Basic Student Ministry in the Kingdom-Focused Church* is a resource for course credit in the subject area "Ministry" of the Christian Growth category of plans. To receive credit, read the book, complete the learning activities, show your work to your pastor, a staff member or church leader, then complete the following information. This page may be duplicated. Send the completed page to:

Christian Growth Study Plan
One LifeWay Plaza
Nashville, TN 37234-0117
FAX: (615)251-5067
Email: cgspnet@lifeway.com

For information about the Christian Growth Study Plan, refer the Christian Growth Study Plan Catalog. It is located online www.lifeway.com/cgsp. If you do not have access to the Internet contact the Christian Growth Study Plan office (1.800.968.551 for the specific plan you need for your ministry.

Basic Student Ministry in the Kingdom-Focused Church
Course Number: LS-0523

PARTICIPANT INFORMATION

Social Security Number (USA ONLY-optional) | Personal CGSP Number* | Date of Birth (MONTH, DAY, YEAR)

Name (First, Middle, Last) | Home Phone

Address (Street, Route, or P.O. Box) | City, State, or Province | Zip/Postal Code

CHURCH INFORMATION

Church Name

Address (Street, Route, or P.O. Box) | City, State, or Province | Zip/Postal Code

CHANGE REQUEST ONLY

☐ Former Name

☐ Former Address | City, State, or Province | Zip/Postal Code

☐ Former Church | City, State, or Province | Zip/Postal Code

Signature of Pastor, Conference Leader, or Other Church Leader | Date

*New participants are requested but not required to give SS# and date of birth. Existing participants, please give CGSP# when using SS# for the first time. Thereafter, only one ID# is required. **Mail to:** Christian Growth Study Plan, One LifeWay Plaza, Nashville, TN 37234-0117. Fax: (615)251-5067.

Rev. 5-02